Change 2.0

Joachim Klewes · Ralf Langen

Editors

Change 2.0

Beyond Organisational Transformation

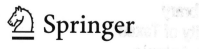 Springer

Professor Dr. Joachim Klewes
Pleon GmbH
Bahnstraße 2
40212 Düsseldorf
Germany
joachim.klewes@pleon.com

Ralf Langen
Pleon GmbH
Theresienhöhe 12
80339 München
Germany
ralf.langen@pleon.com

ISBN 978-3-540-77494-5   e-ISBN 978-3-540-77495-2

DOI 10.1007/978-3-540-77495-2

Library of Congress Control Number: 2007942574

Production: LE-TEX Jelonek, Schmidt & Vöckler GbR, Leipzig
Cover design: WMX Design GmbH, Heidelberg

Printed on acid-free paper

9 8 7 6 5 4 3 2 1

springer.com

Contents

Part II: Insight

Part III: Inside

Part IV: Beyond

Foreword

> "When the winds of change blow, some build walls,
> others build windmills."
> Chinese proverb

Those who want to engage professionally with change management today can choose from a wide range of publications. The available literature on this topic – particularly from the United States and the United Kingdom – fills many metres of shelf space. A Google search for "change management" yields almost two million hits. Readers interested in the topic can find essays and books for practitioners, scientific studies, and firsthand accounts. Given the mass of available information then, it seems reasonable to ask: is another book on change management really necessary?

We asked ourselves this question when we initially developed the concept for this book. Apart from the basic motivation of illuminating the topic from a European and, above all, a communications perspective, we had several reasons for tackling the topic of change.

First, there is the great relevance: today, organisations continuously face the challenge of change, whether they are companies, public bodies, or NGOs. Further, they have to initiate change themselves if they want to get ahead of, or even outlive, their competition. In times of globally networked business processes, accelerated business dynamics, and changing personnel structures, this may seem banal. But in fact, any organisation that closes itself off to change will end up like the dinosaurs, and become extinct. A large capacity and a strong will to change ensure the survival of an organisation. They are the basis for the much-extolled innovative spirit, that everyone likes to claim as their motto. In this sense, they are therefore an important foundation for an organisation's reputation as well.

It is worth noting that the questions that arise when transforming an organisation are no different to those from thirty years ago. Namely, how can organisations shape change so that it has a lasting effect? Can resistance in a company be overcome, and if so, how? What part – if any – should employees play in the process, and how can they be motivated?

Today, the questions are the same. But the answers that managers can and must provide have changed. For example, communication has become more important today. Instead of decrees from management, change today demands complex measures that allow for interaction and ensure transparency. Ideally, there are two main things that change processes must establish internally and externally: motivation and trust. For change, these are essential, as there is often a considerable gap between the wishes of management and the actual attitudes of most staff. This is hardly surprising. If an organisation is going through its fourth, fifth or sixth wave of change, a feeling of indifference (or worse still fear) can take hold. Fear and indifference paralyse an organisation, and can easily cause a transformation to fail.

Organisations that develop, implement and analyse strategies for change today must expend much more effort. And for most change situations, success can only be achieved with the involvement of the employees. The extent to which employees are involved – or more precisely: the extent to which they *feel* involved and taken seriously – decides whether the change succeeds or not.

It's all about the people

To ensure the right degree of employee participation, companies with little or even no experience in change communications often call on external consultants. As Europe's leading communications consultancy (with more than 1,000 employees in 15 key markets), Pleon is in demand as a partner to make change processes successful, and has comprehensive experience. The expertise of the agency is concentrated in the international Change & Transformation practice group.

Making this knowledge and this specifically European perspective available to a wider audience is the second reason for this book. For, the phenomenon of change can best be understood, described and explained on the basis of practical experience. This book is no academic treatise on change management (although some of the authors are, in fact, academics). Rather, it is a collection of articles intended to inspire those involved in the practical implementation of change. Our intention (and hope) is to give the reader food for thought and concrete advice.

For this reason, we include contributions not only from Pleon consultants, but also from other external experts, among them managers of organisations that have experience in managing change. A range of sectors are represented: from industrial companies large and small (in automotives, healthcare, consumer goods and telecommunications) to the public sector.

For all managers who find themselves in similar situations, this 'view from the inside' provides valuable knowledge. For academics engaged in theoretical or empirical research, the articles presented here offer interesting insights that might modify their academic perspectives or suggest new avenues of research. And for students, it may be enriching to learn how change has been managed in actual cases, to counterbalance textbook approaches.

All the authors in this volume agree on one point: successful change is all about the people! This is especially worth noting because, beyond from this common denominator, we have put an emphasis on presenting a diverse range of opinions and experiences. This diversity is the third reason for this book. Among the authors, there are advocates of approaches emphasising employee involvement, those that put a focus on top-down-management, and those somewhere in-between. That there was agreement on the importance of employees prompted us to title the book "Change 2.0" – with a look to the now-established internet trend in which interaction, participation, and democratisation play an important role.

The various perspectives presented in this volume are also the logical consequence of our own experience as consultants working with organisational change. Our experience shows there is no standard solution. Each organisation needs to develop its own approach and its own set of communications measures to change situations.

Our experience also has been incorporated into the development of our change model, which is presented in our article on pages 159 to 181. The model is intended, above all, to help organisations and decision makers distinguish between various kinds of organisational change, while not losing sight of the most important success factor: building trust in a focussed and systematic way.

To illustrate this, we chose a metaphor of five 'expeditions' that organisations in change can embark on. This is an attempt to reduce the complexity of organisational change without being trivial. The metaphors succeed in doing what scientific categories often fail to do: they stimulate discussion among those involved in the change process. And only through discussion, can those involved identify and agree what the basis of their organisation's specific change is, and which factors influence it. We are prepared to accept an inevitable lack of scientific precision in favour of lively debate, or rather, a debate about the right way forward in the given situation.

We hope that the perspectives presented in this book offer the reader a detailed overall picture, and contribute to a deeper understanding of the phenomenon of change. We also hope that this book helps readers to implement change, and successfully use change for their organisation.

Acknowledgements

The power of an anthology such as this depends solely on the strength of the articles in it. Therefore, our thanks firstly go to all the contributing authors. They all have challenging careers that demand intellectual energy and time. Many of our readers will know how challenging it is to work in a job and write an article. This applies especially for articles that leave one open to the criticisms of colleagues or competitors. And for this reason alone, we highly value the contributions of our colleagues.

Were it not for discussions with numerous 'masterminds' at Pleon, especially Timo Sieg, Alex Schoep, Iain Halpin, and also Jan Jelle van Hasselt and Raymond Schra, we would have overlooked a number of important aspects of change. The international book team, led and spurred on by Benedict Winter, not only organised the project, but also vitally contributed to the content and structure – without neglecting their professional commitment to their clients. Particularly worth mentioning here are Kristin Schottmann, Kerstin Steglich, Sabine Stecher and Rudolf-Thassilo Hurth. We are grateful to Anita Schöne and Frauke Witte for typography, typesetting and layout, to Robert Culverhouse and Rowan Payton for translation, and to Daniel Penton for his critical proofreading. Our thanks also go to Dr Niels Peter Thomas of Springer for his patient and helpful guidance.

Special thanks also go to Thomas Fischer, who not only worked unpretentiously behind the scenes to give many of the articles a final polish, but also contributed substantially to the argumentation and formulation of our main article. Without him, this book would not be in your hands.

As always, this project would have been a pipe dream without the understanding and backing of our families. We would therefore like to thank Christina, David, Julian, Sarah and Geraldine as well as Stefanie and Maria.

As the editors of this volume, we of course remain solely responsible for any remaining shortcomings. We therefore welcome your comments, critical or supportive: send us an e-mail to joachim.klewes@pleon.com and ralf.langen@pleon.com.

Joachim Klewes   *Ralf Langen*

Düsseldorf/Munich, January 2008

Incite

Everyone should be dissatisfied with the present situation and should constantly try to improve or change things. It's important to realize that there is always something more we need to aim at. That's what needs to be recognized by every individual. When you're growing you're satisfied with the status quo, and that's no good.

Katsuaki Watanabe, CEO Toyota Motor Corporation, 2005–present

It may come as a surprise: Successful change management is mainly a matter of letting it happen

Paul J. Kohtes

Change is a constant factor in all areas of life – and business is no exception. Proven tools and recognised methods help executives guide their companies through the turbulent tides of change. But the right navigation methods alone are not enough to ensure the success of change processes. Each company or organisation is a vital organism with a heart, soul and identity all of its own. It can be shaped and modified, but cannot be bent without causing damage. At its most effective, change management draws life from the authentic values at the core of the company and its leadership.

"Everything flows and nothing is left unchanged; there is no true state of being, only an eternal becoming and transforming" – this passage, known as the flux doctrine, was written by Plato based on the teachings of Heraclitus. For companies operating under the pressure of globalisation, it has taken on a completely new dynamic. In the maelstrom of virtual information, between mega-mergers and downsizing spirals, only one thing remains certain: business is unpredictable. If you believe Plato, this has always been the case. The apparent slowness of earlier changes simply lulled us into believing we had everything under control and could determine what would happen in the future. Change management marks the departure from this illusion – and at the same time creates a new one: the belief that we only need the right theories and methods to be able to once again steer change along neatly organised tracks.

Targeted changes have long had a firm place on the corporate agenda, and are just as much a part of day-to-day business as are regular meetings of the management board. Two out of three corporations have undergone restructuring processes in recent years. At any given time, at least 40 percent can be found introducing cost-cutting programmes or changing their corporate strategies. Every third company has been faced with sometimes significant changes as a result of mergers or acquisitions (Capgemini 2005). The rate of success, however, is sobering. It can be assumed, for example, that despite high financial outlays and a wide range of flanking measures, about 75 percent of all change projects will not achieve their objectives or will, in fact, fail completely (Vahs and Leister 2003). But why is this the case? Is it because the tools we have are not good enough? Or that executives are not up to the task (anymore)?

Accept change as a constant state

Ideally, a corporate identity takes shape like a river. The bubbling wellspring corresponds to the founding idea of a company. With the first plans and strategies, this spring rapidly gives birth to a stream. As a rule, it develops its own momentum, surging with astonishing dynamism. The direction and goal are not, at first, known quantities. When a company is in its start-up phase, much is still open, faceless and free of tradition. Like a body of water in motion, it reacts to its circumstances and – with the self-assurance of a sleepwalker – always seems to find the best route. From the perspective of a river, there are no change processes, since it owes its entire existence to adaptability – change is its state of being. When we look on in awe at the development of the Chinese economy, we would do well to remember that it owes its momentum to precisely such a "river" mindset. The old Chinese saying, "The heavens are high, the emperor is far away", betrays a lack of concern for central authority that seems at odds with the industriousness and motivation we Westerners expect from the dynamically expanding Asian giant. Yet the power of the Chinese entrepreneurial spirit is undeniable. The corporate identity of a Western company, in contrast, is almost always established on a top-down basis.

Dismantle obstacles

This becomes clear when we take a closer look at a few phenomena that occur during change processes. The annual Gallup polls attest to a pessimistic outlook that has persisted for years at companies in Germany and elsewhere. Only one in ten employees – including more than a few managers – feels allied with his or her employer and is correspondingly motivated. The rest work by the book, at best (Geißler 2006). And there are increasing signs of fatigue even among those who would actually like to show commitment. As a result, emotional problems at the workplace have increased by 70 percent in the last ten years, and every tenth day of absence from work can be attributed to psychological problems (Wirtschaftswoche 2007). Conditions such as these hardly promote the idea of getting involved in something new and viewing change as an opportunity. To put it figuratively, the surging torrent has dwindled into a mere trickle.

Still, only a few top managers recognise these signs of stagnation, often because they concentrate – with great dedication – on sending positive messages to their shareholders. In addition, the relationship to the company's base, and not least to the employees, is easily lost. Where executives address only the public, internal and corporate identification can easily become an empty shell – without any vitality or élan (Deekeling and Arndt 2006). This does not mean there are no managers out there trying very hard to generate shared visions. But their efforts also often lack the natural impetus of water in motion. According to a survey by the German market research institute Forsa, the message of tangible corporate values generally reaches only one out of every three employees (Ligalux 2006).

Change depends on both internal cohesion and openness. When these conditions are less than perfect, only mediocre results can be achieved – even with the best of methods. This is why the first challenge for many executives is to face the facts: a large proportion of employees channel their energies – if at all – in a direction other than that intended by the strategic planning (Kohtes and Rossmann 2006). Change management therefore means first re-establishing a core identity as a credible point of reference. This offers the stability the company needs to undertake change, without robbing it of the flexibility to adapt to varying challenges. This internal alignment cannot function under pressure: if the base resists change, the process will inevitably get bogged down.

Get the current flowing again

Dismantling such an impasse requires reflection on the strengths of a company and its employees. When management is able to get everyone on board, navigation becomes much easier – even in rough seas. True commitment is most likely to develop where true contact takes place and managers do not view their employees as mere subordinates, but as partners to be taken seriously (Buss 2007).

For years, Porsche has successfully demonstrated how a company can persuade not only investors, but also its own employees, despite often problematic market developments. When Porsche boss Wendelin

Wiedeking repeatedly emphasises that employees are among the car-maker's top priorities, this means more than the empty words we are accustomed to hearing. With job guarantees and profit-sharing concepts, the management has demonstrated that change – for many companies, a term synonymous with redundancies or wage cuts – can also be to the advantage of all concerned.

In fact, employee benefits and securities alone are often not even the main source of corporate unity. To flow vigorously, a wellspring needs substantial groundwater to draw on. And a powerful corporate vision shared by all employees and filled with life is a far greater source of impetus than the usual incentive systems – which have been proven to have scant motivating effect anyway. For this reason, companies and organisations must ask themselves a number of key questions. What do we do especially well? Where do we want to go? And what really excites us? At Porsche, the answers read like this:

> Porsche doesn't just build sports cars. Porsche is more. Much more. We love to carry engineering to the extremes. And thereby cut exceptional paths. Our own. Our people are important to us. They sometimes think outside the box. But, above all, they think – creatively and cooperatively. We are constantly in motion. True, we're small – but the Porsche Principle knows no limits. (Porsche 2007)

This is not only a strong vision, but also a set of guidelines for enabling change management.

A key question in this context is "What does the company offer its employees and what does the company expect from them?" After all, a genuine spirit of change can only develop when there is a harmonious relationship between give and take. Some management executives shy away from real transparency in company developments, and keep unpleasant facts a secret for as long as possible. But when businesses finally feel forced to cut a large number of jobs, due to stagnating sales (or in some cases, despite gigantic profits), this is often viewed by the workforce as a lack of honesty. Employees feel demoted to stand-in roles in a change process over which they have no influence. This situation sends negative signals far beyond any individual decision: when managers give the impression that the workforce must passively accept events, employees will remain passive when the next change project arises.

Of course, sometimes it is the employees who reduce themselves to the role of a small cog in a large machine. Those who perceive themselves in this way miss the opportunity to become part of the big picture. It helps if they see work not just as a job or a burden, but as a calling in life. Their ambitions are part of what keeps the river flowing, and everyone – employees and managers alike – must ask themselves from time to time: "Am I still in the right place, with the right company?"

Find your identity and change it constantly

The spirit of change mentioned above cannot be brought about at the push of a button. Like a young plant, it must be watered and perhaps trimmed back from time to time in order to thrive. Classic characteristics such as reliability and courage, independence and passion are the seeds from which the most beautiful flowers grow. However, managers sometimes lose sight of these values, and view change processes as isolated projects to be implemented. They forget that there can be no plant without seeds. Even the best strategies or measures can do little to change this.

Hence, just as a tree doesn't grow in the space of a few days, a company does not become ready for change overnight. Siemens employees, if asked what they think of the change processes implemented in recent years, would likely give different answers from one location to the next. Some business units are still struggling with the latest restructuring measures or fearing further reorganisation, while others are dealing extremely well with change. For example, Siemens Manager Josef Roehrle successfully led the Erlangen electronics plant out of the crisis that it endured in the nineties. Since he took over factory management in 1993, there have been no more redundancies. Change processes are still on the agenda in Erlangen, but Roehrle has created a solid foundation for this: a culture that is created by the people and which therefore takes their needs into account. His principle: no small cogs in a big wheel, but a factory family that has developed over the years (Pletter 2007). For managers, this means not hiding behind methods and projects but dealing with real people and real situations.

Change is a normal occurrence, not an anomaly. However, the very existence of change management shows that this is not accepted in many companies. Those who expect change as part of "business as usual" will find it considerably easier to keep an organisation flowing. A river does not work on a stop-and-go basis – it is in constant motion. If not, it is either jammed or has dried up. But how can this perspective be achieved in practice? Ideas management has placed many companies on the right path. The term itself is part of the solution: whereas change management often generates concerns associated with the need for change, ideas management achieves exactly the opposite. It calls for creativity and design, for involvement and improvement. This is actually how change processes should always be. Recent studies show what potential lies in this shift in perspective. Some sectors are already achieving an employee participation rate of over 40 percent in their ideas management. These changes at the heart of the company easily develop their own natural flow – because they are desired and because their significance is made clear. A positive side effect: the cost-savings potential is huge and even makes other change projects that are working towards the same goal redundant. Deutsche Post AG saved 271 million euros in 2006 thanks to employee suggestions for improvement (Deutsches Institut für Betriebswirtschaft 2007).

Less method, more personality

The route to natural change leads from holding on to power to letting things happen. Just as you cannot tell a river where to flow to, it is also better to give goals as wide a scope as possible in business. Based on this openness, the challenges that arise in each moment can be taken on immediately. Change occurs instead of being initiated by force. But is this a realistic approach?

Google became the global market leader in the online advertising business using exactly this principle. The search engine provider's management leaves its employees to their own devices for ten percent of their working time. During this time, they pursue whatever they consider important. This is exactly how most new Google services are created: they are not planned on the drawing board and no change management is required in order to implement them because they are part of a comprehensive flow principle. Or take Apple. Its days as a company that survived by producing computer hardware alone are long gone. MP3 players and other gadgets are now the main sales drivers at this hotbed of innovation. No change project was required to steer the corporate strategy in a new direction, because the company simply picked up the latest trends time and time again. Apple keeps its finger on the pulse of its market. The word "computer" has since disappeared from the company's name – just like that, without further ado.

This approach to change is not exclusive to the IT sector with its particularly fast innovation cycles. If the corporate culture is right, it works in any context. In a culture of tolerating mistakes and encouraging exploration and discovery, the natural friends of change processes, yet without any explicit change management, Toyota has become the pioneer of environmentally-friendly hybrid motors. At the same time, German carmakers continue to resist the planned tightening of emission legislation, loathing the required modification to their technologies as a troublesome change process.

As the examples show, the less you stand in the way of change, the easier it is to implement. However, this view is an enormous challenge for many managers as it means bidding farewell to the illusion of always having (and always needing to have) things under control. In Taoism, this perspective is called Wu Wei, which essentially means taking action by taking no action. Managers who succeed in distancing themselves from the compulsion to achieve – static – perfection initially find themselves in the middle of nowhere, only to then discover that this opens up the opportunity to do anything. The following Zen story illustrates what is meant by this.

A Zen pupil went to his teacher and asked him: "Do I have to lose my way before I find my destination?" The teacher said: "Now that I no longer have a destination, I don't lose my way any more."

In a business context, this can be understood to mean that targets, not just in change projects, work best when they serve as signposts and do not anticipate the end result, which still lies ahead in the distance. If you view change management as an ongoing dialogue, you always move in step with current challenges and will thus overcome them. In this way, difficulties are not impediments, but rather markers for new directions. Just as a river uses its natural "intelligence" to find the best route, the smartest thing for a company to do is to adopt a more flexible approach to prevailing conditions.

The best way for managers to adopt this open stance is to give their own enthusiasm free rein. This requires self-assurance and the courage to accept the possibility of failure. As the Irish playwright Samuel Beckett once said: "Ever tried. Ever failed. No matter. Try Again. Fail again. Fail better." The departure from the cure-all solution, which usually turns out to be less than a silver bullet in the final analysis anyway, opens up the possibility of achieving the best results offered by each situation.

This has less to do with laissez-faire than with identifying and taking advantage of the opportunities of the moment. When the former Daimler boss Jürgen Schrempp announced the Chrysler takeover, he effectively set off a fireworks display on the stock markets. However, ten years later, his successor Dieter Zetsche was applauded when he indicated that the days of the transatlantic merger could be numbered. What seems right today could be wrong tomorrow. This does not apply to a river. If the water comes up against an obstacle, it simply flows around it. Ideally, daily business life functions according to exactly the same principle. When E.ON finally threw in the towel after more than a year of fighting to take over the energy group Endesa, this did not constitute a failure. Instead, it marked a breakthrough in finding a solution that was far more appropriate for the current conditions.

Outlook

In change management, less is often more. For, change that is organised too strictly usually achieves the opposite and can even paralyse the company. The water in a reservoir only becomes energy once it flows – uninhibited – into the valley. That's why strategies, methods and tools, no matter how important and helpful they may be, are at best aids to support and accompany the natural flow process. Its essence cannot be planned. Letting go does not mean surrendering to challenges. It is the best prerequisite for welcoming change with open arms, courage and enthusiasm.

References

Buss, Eugen (2007) Die deutschen Spitzenmanager. Wie sie wurden, was sie sind. Herkunft, Wertvorstellungen, Erfolgsregeln (in German). Oldenbourg Wissenschaftsverlag, Munich

Capgemini (2005) Veränderungen erfolgreich gestalten. Change Management 2005. Bedeutung, Strategien, Trends (in German) http://www.de.capgemini.com/m/de/tl/Change_Management_2005.pdf (as of: Oct. 2007)

Deekeling, Egbert/Arndt, Olaf (2006) CEO-Kommunikation. Strategien für Spitzenmanager (in German). Campus Verlag, Frankfurt am Main

Deutsches Institut für Betriebswirtschaft (2007) dip-report 2006. Ideenmanagement in Deutschland (in German). Deutsches Institut für Betriebswirtschaft GmbH, Frankfurt am Main

Geißler, Cornelia (2006) Frustfaktor Job (in German). Spiegel Online 31/8/2006. http://www.spiegel.de/wirtschaft/0,1518,434122,00.html (as of Oct. 2007)

Kohtes, Paul J./Rosmann, Nadja (2006) Hören Sie auf zu rennen. Was Manager von Hase & Igel lernen können (in German). J. Kamphausen Verlag, Bielefeld

Ligalux GmbH (2006) Press Release (in German). 21/12/2006

Not Stated (2007) Neue Volkskrankheit: Stress ohne Ende (in German). WirtschaftsWoche 20/3/2007

Pletter, Roman (2007) Systemwechsel (in German). Brandeins 4/2007: 74–89

Porsche (2007) The Porsche Philosophy. http://www.porsche.com/usa/aboutporsche/porschephilosophy/ (as of: Oct. 2007)

Vahs, Dietmar/Leister, Wolf (2003) Change Management in schwierigen Zeiten (in German). Deutscher Universitätsverlag, Wiesbaden

The human factor in change processes: Success factors from a socio-psychological point of view

Marit Gerkhardt, Dieter Frey and Peter Fischer

Why do staff resist change processes? What basic human needs, desires and emotions are behind this resistance? And how can companies take these psychological mechanisms into account in their change projects? The "Model of Twelve Success Factors in Change Processes" reveals how executives can permanently win over their staff to change.

In science and research, change was once a subject primarily reserved for economists, market strategists and the economic sciences. The organisational environment and organisational structures were, and still are, the main focus. Current approaches in industrial, organisational and social psychology, however, substantiate the idea of a further key 'control lever' in change processes – the 'human' factor (Schreyögg 1998, Akademie-Studie, 1999, Greif et al. 2004). Empirical studies show that "changes often fail either because the workforce does not fully understand the purpose of the change, or staff feel overtaxed, or the changes involve exclusively technical, product-related and organisational projects" (Akademie-Studie 1999). Participants in change processes relate the success of a change project to the behaviour and characteristics of the people involved and describe causes unrelated to people as less influential (Greif et al. 2004). In the final analysis, therefore, it is the staff that function as the driving force behind the changes.

Implementation strategies: Top-down or bottom-up?

Irrespective of the reasons for change projects and the type of project, there are two main implementation strategies: "top-down" or "bottom-up" (also called participative) strategies (Gebert and von Rosenstiel 2002). The difference lies in both the initiation and the implementation of the changes. In the "top-down" approach, the changes – e.g. the content, organisation and implementation – are planned and decided by top management, often together with external consultants. The staff are not informed until the changes have been decided on, so that implementation begins immediately. From a psychological point of view, this has drawbacks: staff can easily feel they have no say in the matter and may put up resistance or behave with resignation (von Rosenstiel 1997). The advantage of a "top-down" strategy often lies in time and cost savings, since the changes are decided by a small group beforehand and not in a time and cost-intensive way involving all participants. The clarity of the objective is often described as an advantage. The people affected are told directly where the journey is going in the change process; an image of clear and rigorous management is conveyed.

By contrast, the "bottom-up", or participative, implementation approach directly engages with the affected members of staff. In other words, the people affected become participants and the participants are the people affected. This gives the company management a chance to benefit from their employees' know-how and to simultaneously promote staff motivation through their participation, thus ensuring acceptance of the change (Becker 2001). When people cannot predict or influence events, they experience a loss of control; in a participative and transparent approach, they are more likely to develop a strategy for coping and can also see the positive side of events (Frey and Jonas 2002). This approach is said to have positive effects, for example, in overcoming resistance to innovation, motivating staff and achieving harmony among all members of the organisation (Vroom 1991). Especially in the case of complex tasks, the staff's work performance and level of job satisfaction can be expected to improve if they participate in processing strategies (Antoni 1999).

No unequivocal decision can be made on which of the two implementation strategies is the right one in a specific change process. As a rule, the goal, the timeframes, the background to the process and organisation, and many other aspects have to be taken into consideration. However, psychological literature repeatedly recommends the participative approach, where people have an opportunity to understand the reasoning behind decisions and at the same time voice their opinion and express misgivings and/or counterarguments. For example, people's perception of fairness can be positively influenced (Klendauer and Frey 2005). Finally, the two implementation approaches are not inevitably complementary. In reality there are often transitional or mixed forms of the two strategies (Gebert 2004).

Attitude patterns of the affected staff

The staff are usually the key parameter for the successful implementation of a change project. If we examine the attitude patterns of staff affected by change processes, there is usually a normal distribution, i.e. a few who favour change, a few who reject change and a majority who are sceptical or neutral.

- Those in favour of change can be seen as the spearhead for the implementation of the change: they can hardly wait for the necessary support in order to act. They become active and can be used as multipliers.
- Those that are sceptical or neutral do not really have a well-founded opinion on the change. They have to be positively influenced – i.e. informed, convinced and motivated – with the help of communication and training measures.
- The staff that reject the change, however, are the ones that will strongly resist it. Often, these are people who have been in the company for a long time and want to cling to the status quo (Gairola 2003). It is important to restrict their negative effect.

Causes and forms of resistance

Resistance from the people affected is seen as a decisive challenge for those in charge of change management. What does this resistance involve in concrete terms? As a rule, emotions are in the foreground. Usually, fear is most likely the most important emotion; even the smallest change makes those affected ask: "What does that mean for me or for us?". Change always means leaving behind what we are familiar and comfortable with and facing the unknown. As a rule, the consequences are uncertainty, difficulties and extra effort, so initially, changes often have negative connotations. However, a change only generates fear and stress if people feel there is a threat which they cannot counter (Lazarus 1984). In the context of change processes, stress is often a result of:

- a threat to a person's job or present position
- fear of losing status and esteem
- fear of being unable to keep pace with innovations

According to Lazarus, it is only when the change is not perceived as a danger that the people affected look at its other aspects, for example its usefulness for their own interests or the opportunities. In other words, in change processes, it is important to minimise the threat, to be open about how much an individual will be personally affected, and to encourage open-mindedness towards to the change (Axtell et al. 2002). One possible way to counteract negative attitudes to a change is to announce the imminent innovations openly, honestly and as early as possible – without suppressing any negative aspects. This gives affected people a chance to get accustomed to the change early on. At the same time, possible counter-arguments can be generated in advance and systematically refuted (Frey et al. 2005).

Overall, the findings of psychological research show that resistance is frequently encountered during change processes for no apparent reason. The resistance is either directly related to the person affected or arises within groups or social relations. The type of resistance can tend towards either an active reaction (attack) or a passive reaction (flight) (Table 1). As a rule, resistance is expressed in coded form, e.g. via rumours or power games. In order to be able to counteract this, management must first recognise resistance and the psychological processes on which it is based.

Table 1. Systematic description of typical resistance symptoms

Type of resistance	Individual symptoms	Symptoms in the group/organisation
Active (attack)	• frequent contradiction • counterarguments • criticism of superiors • agitation and complaints • stubborn formalism	• staff members attacking each other personally • clique formation • power games • rumours
Passive (flight)	• absenteeism • slackness, tiredness • inattentiveness • helplessness • working to rule • weakness of character, escape behaviour	• tense atmosphere • inability to make decisions • high illness rate • debates on unimportant issues • high fluctuation rate • lack of cooperation

See Kleist and Maets 2003, based on Doppler et al. 2002.

Why do people react with certain modes of behaviour in certain situations? What needs or emotions are at their core? Answers to these questions can be found in a concept developed by Hron, Frey and Lässig (2005) which is based on people's desires and the relevant psychological theories on how people and groups function. The authors distinguish a total of seven basic needs which have an important influence in change processes (Gerkhardt 2007).

1. Perception of meaning and necessity

According to Schulz-Hardt and Frey's theory of meaning (1997), people fundamentally strive to find meaning in all they experience and do. They long to know the whys and wherefores. The more crucial, unexpected and negative a person feels a circumstance to be, the more urgent is his or her striving to find a meaning. Clarifying and explaining the meaning has a motivating and action-guiding effect. Both the cognitive components (i.e. understanding the purpose) and the affective components (reconciling it with one's personal values) are decisive. How experience is interpreted influences employees' job satisfaction, job motivation and performance, a fact that has been proven by a series of studies in the fields of industrial and organisational psychology (Brodbeck et al. 2002).

2. Transparency and foreseeability

A feeling of transparency and foreseeability is particularly important if people are to react adaptively to complex and uncertain information. Only if they are given this feeling will they recognise the positive aspects of a change in their environment and develop their own strategies for coping with it. If this feeling is lacking, stressful events such as a change in their work situation are likely to be perceived as a loss of control. In this case, fears about their own field of work, job security and organisational identity will stand in the way of a positive development of the change. The consequences will be a low level of emotional well-being and often psychosomatic problems such as sleeping disorders and impaired concentration, which also negatively influence the quantity and quality of work results (Buono and Bowditch 2003).

3. Influenceability and control

People have an increased need for control in unfamiliar and stressful situations. They 'experience' control when they are convinced that they can reduce unpleasant events through their own actions. Control factors include explainability, foreseeability and transparency, influenceability and participation. According to the theory of cognitive control, involving people in processes definitely generates greater identification and willingness to cooperate. Performance can be improved, stress and fear reduced as a result of a perceived influenceability of events (Frey and Jonas 2002). Subjectively experienced control impacts on the degree of identification with the change and on emotional well-being – as shown in an empirical study by Greitemeyer, Fischer, Nürnberg, Frey and Stahlberg on psychological success factors in acquisitions. Here, it becomes clear that the staff in the company that is taken over feel they have less control over their own situation than staff working for the company that is taking them over, and this loss of perceived control in turn leads to a reduction in well-being (Greitemeyer et al. 2006).

4. Perception of the clarity of objectives

People want to know what is happening and where the journey is going. They long for clear objectives. Locke and Latham's goal theory makes it clear that goals have an informational and motivational character. If a goal or a vision is explained, energy, work motivation and performance can be increased considerably (Locke and Latham 1990). To achieve this, the vision must be understood, taken on board and perhaps further developed by the individuals.

5. Equity and fairness

Organisational equity is made up of four components:

- distributive equity
- procedural equity
- interpersonal equity
- informational equity

Distributive equity describes the perceived fairness of results. According to equity theory, people compare their own input and output with the perceived input and output of relevant people in their environment. A feeling of injustice arises if this relation is perceived to be disproportionate. Possible consequences include a reduction in the quality and quantity of work results, a lowering of objectives and an increase in absenteeism (see Müller and Hassebrauck 1993). This feeling can be offset by the other components.

Procedural equity is particularly important in this context. People must understand why a decision has been made. At the same time, they must have a voice, so that they can express any misgivings, scepticism or counterarguments (Klendauer and Frey 2005). This also applies when a decision has already been made. Research into procedural equity tends to emphasise the positive results that can be achieved, such as a positive working atmosphere, trust and loyalty. Meta-analyses show a high correlation between procedural fairness and job satisfaction, performance, organisational commitment and trust (Colquitt et al. 2000, Cohen-Carash and Spector 2001).

In the case of informational and interpersonal equity, the focus is on the communication process. Informational equity is achieved by giving honest and appropriate explanations for the respective decisions. Despite a perceived inequity in the results, acceptance can be achieved if people notice that they have been given negative information just as honestly as positive information.

In the case of interpersonal equity, it is a question of giving people the feeling that they are respected and esteemed. Respectful and correct behaviour towards the people affected gives them the feeling that they are being taken seriously and not instrumentalised.

6. Perception of the benefit of the change

People strive for benefit optimisation in the sense of 'homo oeconomicus'. It is crucial, therefore, that the people affected recognise the benefit and advantage of a change for themselves. If this does not happen, motivation and the willingness to change generally decline. To make the benefit understandable and tangible for the individual, it is a good idea to work out concrete arguments to illustrate the advantages of the change for the staff. This should be followed by an open, direct and broadly based communication of the advantages. It can also be helpful to create specific incentives for the development of the new skills, modes of behaviour or attitudes which are needed for the change: people who develop them will be rewarded, thus increasing their personal benefit. Another important aspect is to generate and reward 'quick wins'.

7. Trust

Trust is an important basis for the successful implementation of organisational changes (Clegg et al. 2002). The extent to which the staff accept their company's ways and suggestions will depend on the extent to which they trust its management. A prevailing level of trust can decisively influence the credibility of explanations as well as the legitimacy of actions (Rousseau and Tijoriwala 1999). In the organisational context, the so-called psychological contract – an unwritten agreement between an organisation's staff and the organisation itself – is also decisive. In this contract, the people affected agree implicitly on important modes of behaviour. If one of the participants violates these implicit expectations, this leads to a feeling of abuse of confidence.

Specialist literature also points out that there are various personality characteristics that influence the way a person deals with organisational changes. A study by Judge et al. (1999) shows, for example, that high levels of self-esteem and risk tolerance have a positive effect on the way people deal with change. However, since personality characteristics can essentially be regarded as stable and difficult to influence, when it comes to the successful management of resistance, the focus tends to lie more on directly applicable measures to promote acceptance.

Twelve success factors in change processes

Against the background of these psychological processes and mechanisms, the question that arises for corporate practice is how the change project should be structured: which concrete factors need to be taken into consideration in order to gain the confidence of the people affected – with their emotions, desires and needs – for the planned change? Time and again the call is heard for a manageable model, a kind of checklist that can act as a guideline for the successful implementation and organisation of a change. Twelve success factors can be identified (Gerkhardt 2007) following comprehensive theoretical research and empirical trials during various corporate change processes (Fig. 1).

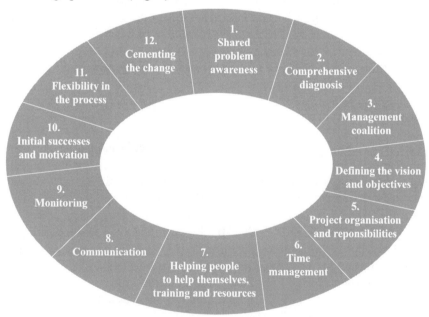

Fig. 1. Model of the twelve success factors in change processes (Gerkhardt 2007)

1. Shared problem awareness

A general, joint awareness of the problem is fundamental to the successful implementation of a change process. In order to achieve this, it is necessary to make the urgency and necessity of the change clear to everyone: people need to be aware of deficits if they are going to be open to innovation and change. Only if there is a shared awareness of the problem and everyone understands the purpose of the change can mental blocks be overcome and fresh energy released for changes.

2. Comprehensive diagnosis

At the beginning of a change project, a comprehensive diagnosis should be made of the status quo. Measures cannot be purposefully planned until the current situation has been assessed – and existing barriers and potential advantages have been recognised and described. Everyone who is affected must be incorporated into a comprehensive and realistic analysis of the situation. This can be done by means of interviews or surveys of a cross-section of people involved.

3. Management coalition

A broad coalition among proponents of the change – i.e. the full backing of top management – is always necessary as a driving and supporting force for the change process. The commitment and credibility of management is decisive, because the willingness of the people affected to accept changes very much depends on how much they trust management. It is important to include further key, responsible people in the lower management levels and other members of staff – in addition to top management – and to use them as multipliers and supporters of the process.

4. Defining the vision and objectives

The objective is defined by means of a vision and concrete subordinate targets. A clear and comprehensible picture of the future creates clarity and indicates the direction in which the journey is going. The vision must be easy to communicate and should be an appeal to stakeholders, staff and customers. The objectives should be as tangible as possible and suitably challenging for the individuals concerned. Furthermore, it is essential to present the objectives in a positive light in view of the imminent change, so that the people affected are motivated and have an interest in supporting and implementing the vision.

5. Project organisation and responsibilities

Basic factors affecting the success of a project include professional project organisation with staff that are trained professionally, methodologically and psychologically, and the clear definition of roles and responsibilities. The need for a basis of trust among the people involved must be taken into account when setting up the project organisation. If possible, the organisation should already include representatives of the various target groups of the change. Since they will frequently be deployed as multipliers or communicators, they must be credible and trustworthy and have expertise and knowledge of the subject matter. Staff willingness to change their attitudes or develop new ones can be considerably influenced in this way (Frey et al. 2005). Towards the end, an "extended" project organisation can be used to encourage and guarantee the participation of the people involved throughout the process, so that all points of view are taken into consideration.

6. Time management

Every change project should be planned systematically and with a realistic time framework. Detailed planning helps to keep the process under control and makes it possible to intervene and make timely changes. It is important here to allow enough time for the implementation and stabilisation of the change. By communicating and informing everyone involved about the time framework for coordination and planning, for example with project plans showing dates and deadlines, the people affected can develop a 'change script' of the content and times and adapt to the subsequent changes.

7. Helping people to help themselves, training and resources

The necessary resources – for example, human resources, time and budget – have to be available if the people affected are to be energised and motivated for the change process. Furthermore, the participants have to be given support, especially in the fields of training and qualifications. Encouragement in the form of advice, feedback, leadership, and so forth can make an important contribution. It is important to give the people affected an opportunity to actively participate in the change and thus make their own contribution to successful implementation.

8. Communication

Regular and interactive exchanges of information and ideas, and systematic, comprehensive communication, are indispensable for every change process. This can help create trust and have a positive influence on people's openness to change. All available communication channels should be used to ensure lively and comprehensive communication; in practice, direct, one-to-one conversations are often the most successful method. It is important to communicate in good time, on a broad level, and in an open, clear and lively manner. 'In good time' means that communication should begin as early as possible to prevent possible rumours and uncertainties surfacing. 'On a broad level' means that all target groups affected must be included in communication. 'Open' means that fair communication also involves truthfully passing on bad news. 'Clear' communication means using the language of the people affected to encourage conversations on equal terms and create confidence.

9. Monitoring

Monitoring – in the sense of continuously accompanying and evaluating a change process – forces those in charge to clearly define objectives already in the run-up to the project and helps them recognise, in good time, if the project is becoming stagnant or moving in the wrong direction. As a result, it is important that monitoring is not only carried out after the change, but continuously tracks the entire process. Professional monitoring takes into account not only the 'hard factors', such as milestones and defined corporate ratios, but also 'soft factors', for example the participants' satisfaction and motivation levels.

10. Initial successes and motivation

The implementation of a change frequently requires a considerable amount of time; the same applies to the first noticeable successes. Yet the latter are particularly important in the execution of a change project for maintaining the necessary energy levels on the part of all participants. Initial successes show the people affected that things really can be shifted, thus confirming their commitment and initiative. Recognisable successes create a positive overall mood and release new motivation and energy. Another important motivating factor is continuous appreciation and rewards for achievements.

11. Flexibility in the process

Change projects quite often have to flexibly take renewed changes into account – even during the implementation stage. For example, the company or customer might develop new requirements in the course of the process which require a quick reaction from the company. Similarly, additional training courses or other support measures may become necessary in the course of the change process. There are innumerable examples of these and similar circumstances cropping up in practice; they show that a certain degree of flexibility should be always maintained, especially in detailed operational planning (Doppler and Lauterburg 2002).

12. Cementing the change

The stability of a change's success always depends on how well it has become established and secure. The new approaches, procedures and modes of behaviour can be consolidated either formally as written rules, tasks and workflows or in the form of a redefined vision. The bottom line is to provide convincing leadership, giving priority to permanently stabilising the changes. Furthermore, steps should be taken to ensure the continuation of the change by the subsequent management generation, in order to consolidate the changes that have been taught or implemented (Kotter 1995).

The twelve success factors illustrate the many different levels and measures that need to be taken into consideration within a change process. A comprehensive empirical analysis has confirmed that all the above factors are relevant for the successful implementation of a change process (Gerkhardt 2007). However, different success factors can take on a key role, depending on the project background.

Conclusion

In practice, a question that quickly arises is: "Who is responsible for the successful implementation of a change project and for ensuring the key success factors?" Even though the initiators, for example the executive board, are ultimately at the top of the list, and professional consultants may be very much involved, in the final analysis it is the directly responsible project or line managers who have responsibility as the drivers and implementers of the change. Consultants can certainly take on an important support function, for example in the often critical diagnosis of the current situation and in gaining an objective picture of views of the people affected. However, responsibility for ensuring the success factors are realised is in practice borne by the responsible managers (Gerkhardt 2007).

Accordingly, these days a good executive also has to be a good change manager. For, due to the great general pressure to change, handling and successfully managing changes has become an essential task in almost all areas and is now almost a manager's "daily bread" (Reiss et al. 1997). The main requirements, for example, are knowing the expectations of the staff, reacting to them promptly and, if necessary, counteracting them. Executives increasingly have to deal with uncertainties, yet they still have to make resolute decisions. Many authors refer to the participation and support of all staff as a major success factor (Sandau and Jöns 2001). Executives and managers must aim at encouraging and demanding top performance of their staff – using all their staff's talents, abilities and interests. Holding feedback meetings and target-agreement meetings, helping people to help themselves, maximising communication, and setting an example – all these are indispensable (Frey et al. 2004).

In view of these requirements, it becomes clear that differentiated training measures for executives in the field of change management are more necessary than ever. In order to be able to deal successfully with change almost on a daily basis, it is vital for an executive not to be just superficially concerned with strategies or measures, but to understand the background issues, i.e. essential psychological processes and emotions (Gerkhardt and Frey 2006). Only when these are internalised does it become possible to successfully realise the key success factors.

References

Akademie-Studie (1999) Warum Veränderungsprojekte scheitern (in German). Unreleased results of a study done by the academy for executives. Bad Harsburg. http://www.die-akademie.de (as of: Feb. 2006)

Antoni, C. H. (1999) Konzepte der Mitarbeiterbeteiligung: Delegation und Partizipation (in German). In: Graf Hoyos, C./Frey, D. (eds) Arbeits- und Organisationspsychologie. Psychologische Verlagsunion, Weinheim, pp 569–583

Axtell, C./Wall, T./Stride, C./Pepper, K./Clegg, C./Gardner, P./Bolden, R. (2002) Familiarity Breeds Content: The Impact of Exposure to Change on Employee Openness and Well-Being. Journal of Occupational and Organisational Psychology, 75: 217–231

Becker, L. (2001) Personalabteilung im Unternehmenswandel – Anforderungen, Aufgaben und Rollen im Change Management (in German). Deutscher Universitätsverlag, Wiesbaden

Brodbeck, F./Maier, G./Frey, D. (2002) Führungstheorien (in German). In: Frey, D./Irle, M. (eds) Theorien der Sozialpsychologie. Bern: Huber, Band II, pp 327–363

Buono, A./Bowditch, J. (2003) The Human Side of Mergers and Acquisitions: Managing Collisions between People, Cultures and Organisations (2nd. ed.). Beard Books, pp 108–133

Clegg, C./Unsworth, K./Epitropaki, O./Parker, G. (2002) Implicating Trust in the Innovation Process. Journal of Occupational Psychology, 75: 409–422

Colquitt, J.A./Conlon, D.E./Wesson, M. J./Porter, C.O./Ng, K.Y. (2001) Justice at the Millennium: A Meta-analytic Review of 25 Years of Organisational Justice Research. Journal of Applied Psychology, 86: 425–445

Doppler, K./Lauterburg, C. (2002) Change Management: Den Unternehmenswandel gestalten (10. Auflage) (in German). Campus, Frankfurt am Main

Frey, D./Greitemeyer, T/Fischer, P. (2005) Einstellungen (in German). In: Frey, D./v. Rosenstiel, L./ Graf Hoyos, C. (eds) Wirtschaftspsychologie. Beltz, Weinheim, pp 55–60

Frey, D./Peus C./Jonas E. (2004) Soziale Organisationen als Center of Excellence mit Menschenwürde – Zur Professionalisierung der Mitarbeiter- und Unternehmensführung (in German). In: Maelicke, B. Personal als Erfolgsfaktor. Nomos, Baden-Baden, pp 27–52

Frey, D./Jonas, E. (2002) Die Theorie der kognisierten Kontrolle (in German). In: Frey, D./Irle, M. (eds) Theorien der Sozialpsychologie (Band III). Motivations-, Selbst- und Informationsverarbeitungstheorien. Huber, Bern, pp 13–50

Gairola, A. (2003) Das Unternehmen umbauen (in German). Harvard Business Manager, 10/03: 61–80

Gebert, D. (2004) Organisationsentwicklung (in German). In: Schuler, H. (ed), Lehrbuch Organisationspsychologie. Huber, Bern, pp 601–616

Gebert, D./v. Rosenstiel, L. (2002) Organisationspsychologie (in German). Kohlhammer, Stuttgart, pp 401–410

Gerkhardt, M. (2007) Erfolgsfaktoren und Bewertungskriterien in Change Management Prozessen. Mehrebenenanalyse von drei Veränderungsprozessen innerhalb eines internationalen Automobilherstellers (in German). Dr. Kovac, Hamburg

Gerkhardt, M./Frey, D. (2006) Erfolgsfaktoren und psychologische Hintergründe in Change Prozessen – Entwicklung eines integrativen psychologischen Modells (in German). Zeitschrift für Organisationsentwicklung, 04/2006: 48–59

Greif S./Runde B./Seeberg I. (2004) Erfolge und Misserfolge beim Change Management (in German). Hogrefe, Goettingen

Greitemeyer, T./Fischer, P./Nürnberg, C./Frey, D./Stahlberg, D. (2006) Psychologische Erfolgsfaktoren bei Unternehmenszusammenschlüssen (in German). Zeitschrift für Arbeits- und Organisationspsychologie, 50, 01/06: 9–16

Hron, J./Lässig, A./Frey, D. (2005) Change Management – Gestaltung von Veränderungsprozessen (in German). In: Frey, D./v. Rosenstiel, L./Hoyos, C. (eds) Wirtschaftspsychologie. Beltz Verlag, Weinheim, Basel, pp 120–124

Judge, T./Thoresen, C.J./Pucik, V./Welbourne, T.M. (1999) Managerial Coping with Organisational Change: A Dispositional Perspective. Journal of Applied Psychology, 84: 107–122

Kleist, S./Maets, H. (2003) Widerstände im Change-Management (in German). In: Schewe, G. Change-Management – Facetten und Instrumente. Dr. Kovac, Hamburg, pp 53–68

Klendauer, R./Frey, D. (2005) Fairness bei Prozessen (in German). In: Frey, D./v. Rosenstiel, L./Graf Hoyos, C.(eds) Wirtschaftspsychologie. Beltz, Weinheim, pp 92–95

Kotter, J.P. (1995) Leading Change. Why Transformation Efforts Fail. Harvard Business Review, 73, pp 59–67

Lazarus, R.S. (1984) Psychological Stress and the Coping Processes. McGraw-Hill, New York

Locke, E. A./Latham, G.P. (1990) A Theory of Goal Setting and Task Performance. Prentice Hall, Englewood Cliffs, N. J.

Müller, G./Hassebrauck, M (1993) Gerechtigkeitstheorien (in German). In: Frey, D./Irle, M. (eds) Theorien der Sozialpsychologie. Huber, Bern, Volume I, pp 217–240

Reiß, M./v. Rosenstiel, L./Lans, A. (1997) Change Management. Programme, Projekte und Prozesse (in German). Schäffer-Poeschel, Stuttgart

v. Rosenstiel L. (2003) Arbeits- und Organisationspsychologie – Wo bleibt der Anwendungsbezug? Mannheimer Beiträge zur Wirtschafts- und Organisationspsychologie (in German). 02/03, 15–20

v. Rosenstiel, L. (1997) Verhaltenswissenschaftliche Grundlagen von Veränderungsprozessen (in German). In: Reiß, M./v. Rosenstiel, L./Lans, A. (eds) Change Management. Programme, Projekte und Prozesse. Schäffer-Poeschel, Stuttgart, pp 191–212

Rousseau, D. M./Tijoriwala, S. A. (1999) What's a Good Reason to Change? Motivated Reasoning and Social Accounts in Promoting Organisational Change. Journal of Applied Psychology, 84: 514–528

Sandau, M./Jöns, I. (2001) Die Auswirkung der Veränderungsbereitschaft des Managements auf das Veränderungserleben der Mitarbeiter (in German). Mannheimer Beiträge zur Wirtschafts- und Organisationspsychologie, 03/01, pp 15–24

Schreyögg, G. (1998) Organisation. Grundlagen moderner Organisationsgestaltung. 2. Auflage (in German). Gabler, Wiesbaden, pp 485–551

Schulz-Hardt, S./Frey, D. (1997) Das Sinnprinzip: Ein Standbein des Homo Psychologicus (in German). In: Mandl, H. (ed) Bericht über den 40. Kongress der Deutschen Gesellschaft für Psychologie. Hogrefe, Goettingen, pp 870–876

Vroom, V.H./Arthur, G.J. (1991) Flexible Führungsentscheidungen. Management der Partizipation in Organisationen (in German). Poeschel, Stuttgart, pp 10–22

Accelerated change dynamics within the healthcare industry: Just a trend, or is there more to it?

Markus Pickel

Reports of mergers and corporate takeovers have featured regularly in the press for years now. Buzzwords like 'merger waves' and 'mega-mergers' point to developments that evidently occur repeatedly world-wide but differ greatly from sector to sector. Over the last few years, this has led to a considerable change in the competitive landscape, particularly in the healthcare industry. One of the main causes of this has been − and still is − a radical transformation of business models driven by changes in demographic conditions and rising costs in healthcare systems, most of which are state-controlled. The kind of free market forces that dominate other industries are of little meaning here. The business development and business models of the providers of medicines and health services are under great pressure to change, not only from the classic 'customers' (prescribing doctors, pharmacists), but also from insurers and the respective governments − through regulation and intervention in the market. This affects both classic pharmaceutical companies and healthcare service providers.

The time cycles of such changes have been becoming ever shorter in recent years. Today, many major companies no longer rely solely on classic departments such as product development and sales, they also have highly specialised members of staff who focus on the purchase and sale side of business operations, product knowledge and rights. A closer look at the successful players in the pharmaceutical industry reveals that it is by no means rare for a company to have changed its portfolio by up to 60 percent over a period of three to five years. The following contribution deals with an essential success factor in steering such change processes: the "speed and decisiveness" factor.

High level of change dynamics within the healthcare industry

Patent terms last 20 years. The necessary clinical tests take an average of eight years, and approval procedures about another two. So, the effective exploitation period of a patent is less than ten years. These days, the cost of developing a promising new drug can reach a staggering one billion US dollars. The sector is therefore permanently battling with a high level of pressure to innovate on the one hand, and much more stringent prerequisites for approval and cost reimbursement on the other, as illustrated by discussions on sham innovations. At the same time, the protection of intellectual property in the growth markets of Asia and Latin America is repeatedly the subject of discussion. This forces companies to seek high profitability margins, which in turn leads to public criticism, especially in times of empty public coffers.

Companies with a high proportion of blockbusters (medicines or products with an annual turnover of a billion dollars or more) in particular have to make detailed, targeted plans for the future. This is because the loss of patent protection usually leads to immediate revenue and profitability losses of between 60 and 80 percent. Examples from the last few years clearly illustrate the direct link between a well-filled (or empty) 'product pipeline' and a company's share price or market value. Hoechst/Aventis and Pfizer are well-known examples for this, although medium-sized providers are also affected. If a blockbuster has to be withdrawn, or if a product fails at a late development phase (Phase III), a crisis scenario of undreamt-of proportions can develop overnight.

This is the real reason why this type of company particularly needs a lot of expertise in change management and communication – and why some of them have indeed developed such skills. However, since the companies themselves are often overstretched in such situations, a highly specialised brand of professional service providers has emerged in the field of communications and 'change consulting'. Their value for the companies is undisputed. The time factor means more than money, especially in these situations: it can decide whether a change succeeds – or fails, with often dramatic consequences for the company's stakeholders. This applies to critical change processes, but also to all other major change situations (mergers, acquisitions, portfolio streamlining, major restructuring or reengineering programmes): maximum speed and decisiveness are required at all times.

Why are change programmes more in demand today than ever before?

Since Aventis was taken over by Sanofi a few years ago, European companies have predominantly been the driving force in mergers in the pharmaceutical sector. The background to this development is the pent-up demand in the European pharmaceutical industry, which is still much more fragmented than its counterpart in the United States.

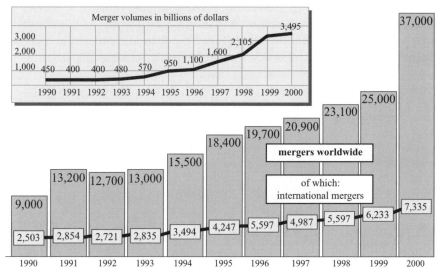

Fig. 1. Mergers: A flourishing marriage market for companies (Sources: UNCTAD, Securities Data, Computasoft Research/Commscan, Institut der deutschen Wirtschaft, Cologne)

Bayer group's takeover of Schering AG in 2006 began a trend towards mergers among medium-sized companies. The providers of products for specialist physicians ("specialty care pharmaceuticals") in particular are very much in demand, since their risk profile is lower than that of marketing-intensive primary-care providers, which are highly dependent on blockbusters. The creation of Bayer Schering Pharma was quickly followed by numerous other corporate mergers in Europe. One was triggered when the patents ran out on two of Belgian group UCB's top-selling products. By purchasing Schwarz Pharma in 2006, UCB was able to bolster its own development pipeline and above all, build up its position in the field of neurological illnesses. Merck Serono followed this example. And the trend is continuing: the pharmaceutical group AKZO sold its health business to the American company Schering Plough in 2007.

Portfolio – Process – People: The trinity of speed in change

Although media coverage and the increasingly global dimensions of change processes create the impression that the situation is more acute these days, in fact change processes have always been part of our economic and social life. What is new, above all, is their increasing frequency (see Fig. 1) and the acceleration of the respective changes that result. Strengthened by growing transparency and publicity, three core factors in change processes must therefore be identified as quickly as possible and adapted to this new (time) context (Fig. 2): portfolio, process and people. Speed is required here, otherwise change dynamics can quickly falter.

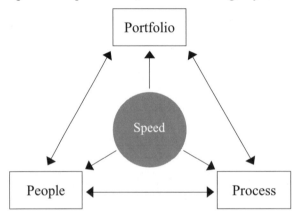

Fig. 2. Parameters for successful change processes

Portfolio summarises the new corporate strategy including its decisions on the company's range of services, as well as its fundamental orientation and guiding principles. Particularly in merger situations and in the context of acquisitions, both investors and the company's own staff demand clear answers in this area. Growth alone is not enough, either for the capital market or for the staff and customers: the often-quoted formula "1+1 > 2" usually raises more questions than it answers. The quick decisions are almost impossible to explain to the respective target groups unless the companies are really logical in the way they argue their corporate strategy and demonstrate excellent communication skills.

For example, Bayer's acquisition of Roche's OTC division in 2004 impressively showed how competitiveness in the consumer-care market could be significantly improved within a short period; the swift communication of a corresponding corporate story focusing on the 'portfolio' ensured broad acceptance among the stakeholders. There has been considerable further consolidation in this sector since then (Boots/Reckitt Benkiser, Pfizer/J&J). This has ecouraged a high level of change dynamics and demands a credible portfolio strategy that needs to be convincingly communicated.

The management of the **processes** in the new company, or new corporate unit, and the operating models behind it, represent a key success factor, particularly in the case of corporate mergers or significant portfolio changes. Great speed is required, not only for the processes themselves, but also for their analysis, structuring and implementation. However, great care is needed at the same time, because this is where the blueprint of the new company is created. The processes themselves are in a continuous state of flux and are thus a main factor generating the need for "speed". The timing of the activities is a decisive factor which determines whether a change process succeeds or fails.

Increasing dynamics always means acceleration, too. To give an example from corporate communications, it used to take several days before an edited manuscript arrived back at an internal editor's desk – having been sent by internal mail to the typing pool. Today the finished text is back in the sender's email inbox within a maximum of a few hours. The conclusion is that both internal and external services (e.g. a frequent traveller printing out his ticket on his own printer) have accelerated substantially. This applies not only internally, but also externally, especially in dealing with modern media such as news agencies and radio/TV. The Internet has exponentially accelerated information processes. At the same time, new trends, such as weblogs, have made it even more difficult to control information processes.

However, acceleration not only consists in simply speeding up the completion of individual tasks that have always been done. The focus is rather on achieving a substantial acceleration by acting in an innovative, creative manner, thus achieving a change in the company's processes – for example, in order to drastically reduce the 'time to market'.

'Generating speed' is not least a question of target-oriented time allocation. Enough time must be available for creative processes, for change activities and change communication at the various corporate levels. The third factor – "**People** Management" – therefore is of particular importance.

In order to secure the success of the change, it is absolutely essential to have members of staff who are autonomous, flexible, ready-to-learn, broadly trained, highly motivated and creative. They must break down (and rebuild) structures, question rules, recognise connections between disciplines and be able to act holistically. Employees who have only learned to move within traditional hierarchies and to use them to further their own careers, who have only been receiving and carrying out orders for decades and have had little scope to make their own decisions – will not be prepared for these enormous demands. People prefer stable conditions, familiar environments and well-signposted roads which they can follow safely. The order and stability patterns that often still prevail in companies are no longer suitable for the dynamic, ever-accelerating challenges which result, for example, from the need to cooperate around the globe in virtual, non-hierarchical teams.

To this extent, a dramatic change in processes is often unavoidable – especially when change situations first crop up – and this also destabilises existing conditions, leading to a deterioration of performance. However, rules have to be broken if instability is to be deliberately generated to create change dynamics. Change management needs this kind of breaking of rules ("we've always done it this way" is no longer the norm), irritation (the new boss in jeans) and upheavals (the dress code is unrecognisable) in order to break out of structures that have become fossilised. However, since most rules are observed or obeyed unconsciously, changing the corporate cultures in companies that have always obeyed such rules must be approached extremely sensitively. The strategic management of instability is a real art.

As part of the change process, corporate culture in particular exerts a decisive influence as a value-driving element of the change process and thus on the people living with it and within it. If they are motivated and are integrated into the company where they work, they will be more willing to serve this company and will thus be more productive than colleagues who just feel like a cog in a wheel and are so demotivated that they cannot wait to clock out every afternoon. As a result, corporate culture is the "way we do things here", i.e. the way people work in a company. Common values, experiences, attitudes and modes of behaviour that are shared by all members of staff, characterise the day-to-day working routine just as much as the company's outward image.

The aim must therefore be to develop an understanding for the employees' preferences and behaviour patterns – but to simultaneously establish the changing of these patterns as a fixed component of the corporate culture. This is why change processes differ so dramatically from one company to another. For example, whereas a rapid decision-making process might be accepted as a reality in the departments of one company because 'the team' is used to it from their superior, the same decision-making process might progress totally differently in a comparable company, because the people there deal with the required decision differently. Speed here is a quantity that is always dependent on other variables, particularly on the attitudes and motivation of the protagonists involved.

Staff cannot be expected to be flexible and open in the way they deal with changes if they have no idea why this is being demanded of them. Things are made worse by fears and worries if the staff suddenly realise that they are not (or no longer) up to the pressure and speed of the change mechanisms. Laissez-fair behaviour patterns among top managers are often an indication of this – leading to confusion among the staff.

Particularly during complex change phases, quick decisions have to be taken within a very tight schedule; ideally, many – but rarely all – employees will understand why these decisions have to be taken. The desire for reliable and secure leadership from superiors and top managers is especially pronounced during these phases. If this need for reliability and security is not met, it is a good idea to "decelerate" the change process to prevent the system descending into total chaos. Only in this way will it be possible to become even quicker at the decisive moment.

A digression concerning the real power of corporate culture

Corporate culture is never static; it is constantly in motion in the same way that the company and the people working for it are in a constant process of development. The way that individuals work towards the targets of their team, businesses unit and company; the style of leadership that they expect from their superiors or practise themselves; how customer-oriented, ready to compromise or decisive the staff are in their work; how well communication or mistakes are handled – all these (in short: corporate culture) are decisive factors for business success.

When several corporate cultures come together, for example in the case of mergers or acquisitions, an integrative approach to finding a common culture will normally be tried, simply in order to improve communicability. The aim is to develop a new, independent corporate culture containing elements of both organisations. One reason why this culture model is most likely to succeed is that all the people involved are most likely to cooperate when it comes to the need for swift implementation. This is because – at least from a superficial viewpoint – fewer groups will be disadvantaged than, for example, in other culture models in which either one company gives up (or has to give up) its cultural independence or both cultures continue to exist, in which case people's ties with their respective former company will remain very pronounced.

However, any plans to implement new elements of a corporate culture quickly, will run into problems if the company attempts to force a new culture onto the staff, i.e. if it is not adapted to the actual conditions. Culture changes cannot be ordered – they often take years to implement. One commonly observed mistake is that a company's staff are not given enough time to get accustomed to new patterns of thought and action. But if a person is simply 'ordered' to work in new ways without being convinced of what she or he is doing, many well-intentioned projects will come to nothing. Unless the responsible people are conscious that the key spark of leadership comes from their 'practising' corporate culture, the staff will most likely work listlessly and without orientation – despite all the glossy brochures explaining corporate values that they might receive.

The cultural change process therefore needs to be given enough time. For all the speed and decisiveness with which the elementary components of the new corporate culture must be formulated, their communication, modification and implementation require a lot of time; how long will depend on the size of the company. Even with massive assistance from external consultants, large, globally-oriented groups often need two to three years before they have given all their top managers and staff on all continents the three or four workshops or training courses needed to really acquaint them systematically with the new culture patterns. Intercultural management is consequently always required in the headquarters; what is not needed is an insistence on independence.

In view of the importance of change programmes for the bottom line, neither the personnel department nor corporate communications must be left in exclusive control. If the company management does not credibly stand at the head of the change movement and practise this credibly for the staff, failure is inevitable.

Corporate communications as the mediator of change

The staff are not the only stakeholders who are directly or indirectly affected by change processes. Major changes in a company impact on all stakeholders: management, the staff and their families, the neighbourhoods and communities where the branches are located, customers and suppliers, public authorities and politicians, the shareholders and opinion leaders, as well as the media.

Table 1. Stakeholders and their expectations.

Stakeholders	Expectation relating to ...
Leadership level/top management	• revenue growth and profits • control and power functions • status • career • scope for creative freedom • remuneration
Staff	• job guarantees • career opportunities • work processes • quality of work • security of locations
Public in the neighbourhood/branch location	• consequences for the region • promises made by management • job security
Customers and suppliers	• existing business relations • adherence to contracts • quality standards
Public authorities and politicians	• legal consequences (cartel laws) • increase in the number of unemployed • environmental consequences • tax receipts
Shareholders/financial markets	• increase in the company's value • management's assertive ability • company strategy and structure • product portfolio

Top managers have top responsibility

Top managers are the helmsmen of their company. However, without direct or indirect communication they can neither set the course nor hold it. During change phases, executive and middle management need to be even better at carrying out their responsibility to communicate than under calmer conditions. The only kind of person who can exercise leadership is someone who nails his or her colours to the mast and faces up squarely to all the issues involved – even in precarious situations like when a company lays off workers.

The staff must get a sense that the management are doing justice to their leadership function and are involving them in the changes by letting them contribute their opinions and ideas without fear of sanctions. A combination of these top-down and bottom-up processes help synchronise entrepreneurial willingness with personal willingness to engage in change. No dialogue is possible without trust on both sides – although it is management's responsibility to build up credibility and trust to form a solid basis for cooperation. The expertise of the internal communication specialists is needed here; they must take 'their' CEO or board team to the places and into the divisions where the need is most urgent. Roadshows, kick-off events and leadership meetings are examples of venues where company executives can appeal for trust and, conversely, where they can enter into a dialogue, in order to make progress on all aspects of change communication.[1]

Quick decisions must be discussed in detail and coordinated appropriately. This 'getting-to-the-heart-of-things' aspect of opinion-forming and selection processes (Who is the new boss? Who is in charge on the first and second levels?) and the subsequent practical implementation – with (new) members of staff taking up new positions and other staff leaving the company – must be irreversible. Nothing is more dangerous and less convincing in change processes than sudden reversals of decisions that have already been communicated. Here, the "speed" factor must be treated with particular sensitivity, because the quick decisions are not always the right ones. The staff must also be informed if important decisions are still pending. Here it is not so much the content of the information that is important, rather the fact that people are informed about the status quo regularly and in short intervals. "Process information" is the term for this strategy of at least communicating the time and mode of decision-making, even when there is no news of substance to communicate.

The focus is on the staff

PR begins at home: only if managers openly supply comprehensive information within the company can they, conversely, expect others to trust them. The right kind of communication with the employees' representatives is of key importance in this context. They should be immediately integrated into the dialogue process (especially, of course, in countries with strict laws on co-determination) without holding back important information. The company's works council, as management's link with the workers, is an important partner in specific change situations, precisely because the aim is to accelerate work sequences. The initial communication proc-

---

[1] See Katrin Schwabe's contribution in this volume for more information on dialogue formats.

esses can be sped up considerably (for example, by convening company meetings with all staff; providing staff with coordinated information; making use of synergy effects etc.) if management put their cards on the table in the internal dialogue with the employees' representatives; in other words, if the emphasis is placed on openness and mutual trust.

Staff must be approached differently during change phases than they would be in routine communication. Faster media such as special newsletters (both print and electronic versions) are needed here. The individual steps within a change project can serve as a 'checklist' for the individual information components (What changes were targeted? What results have been achieved? What is our current position? What milestones lie behind us? What milestones lie ahead?). Furthermore, information via the intranet and integration websites dealing exclusively with change topics (for example, in the context of a corporate merger), and 'questions of the day' are tried-and-tested tools for providing answers to important questions, especially in unstable and uncertain situations.

The faster, the better, should be the objective during this communication phase. For corporate mergers in particular, it is important to synchronise the communication channels in both original companies: on the one hand to document the fact that all the information comes 'from a single source', even if the implementation phase is still running or if there are unanswered legal questions, and on the other hand because quickly-made decisions prepare future communication channels and outline responsibilities and structures. Means of communicating rules (staff newspaper, manager's letters, etc.) can also help supply the workforce with important, up-to-date information.

The local population are curious

The neighbourhood at corporate locations must be informed just as quickly and professionally as the company's own employees. Nothing is more difficult than reacting to rumours and 'truths' that have already been published in the printed media. In the run-up to important decisions affecting the location (relocation of production, adjustments in production capacity or the future number of jobs), the public must be informed about the details that are important for them. Whether precise figures etc. are already available is secondary here; the important thing is to provide swift information about trends. Otherwise rumours and speculation will spread though the town like wildfire – and then it will be too late to correct them.

Customers and suppliers are partners

No company can exist without customers and suppliers. Yet this truism only becomes really relevant when the two groups start asking critical questions about whether or how the changes are of importance for business relations, for example, whether quality is expected to decline or whether customers will continue to enjoy top priority in company service. Here, letters to customers and suppliers are useful means of proactive communication. Rapid feedback analyses and surveys of customers and suppliers also help a company to keep its finger on the market's pulse. Selected customer groups are surveyed at certain intervals (merger announcement, integration phase, new company). Possible methods include invitations to customers, customer forums on the Internet, feedback surveys and inquiries by telephone.

Public authorities and politicians need information

Especially in times of mergers and acquisitions, politicians must nail their colours to the mast to supply their voters with information. In this context, the message that politicians – whichever party they belong to – always want to send to their electorate is: "Your job is safe". In most cases, such catchy phrases are not appropriate; when changes are planned, particularly in the context of mergers, the main and most discussed issues are always the number of job losses and job relocations.

The shareholders as external customers

Only one thing counts for shareholders: will the announced measures and changes increase the company's value, or are there fears that the corporate strategy will not have the desired effect? The day-to-day share prices of many companies give tangible proof of how a company is performing. Here, also, corporate communications must focus on providing the shareholders and analysts with the most important and up-to-date key data as quickly as possible.

One important issue in all change processes in this context is the composition and selection of management: if the (new) management does not inspire confidence, this can sometimes have swift consequences – and can even lead to their replacement. Regular (electronic) shareholders' newsletters and other information that is relevant for analysts are examples of target-group-oriented means of communication. Above all, however, an ongoing dialogue, analysts' meetings and get-togethers with the media that are important for the capital market are also helpful for communicating important information and picking up feedback.

Getting the timing right is the top priority for all stakeholders

The 'time' and 'topicality' factors are therefore important for all the above-mentioned stakeholders. They must be informed about the planned changes quickly and at the right time for each group. Whenever time differences are relevant – because of regional differences at international locations – local managers must take over the headquarters' communication tasks. This means that all the relevant companies in the various countries must be given individual communication plans in line with their respective regional situation. Getting the timing right and using fast coordination channels are the most important success criteria when disseminating news.

A second wave of communication (in the case of mergers) contains the information on the respective overall conditions, weighted specifically for each stakeholder group. To this purpose, change plans should be available containing statements that vary in terms of time and content. They should focus on providing, at short intervals, the individual groups with information that is as up-to-date as possible. During this wave, the staff are the group that has to be 'supplied' with change communication for the longest period. Indeed, it is common for this period to last three or four years.

Change communication as a key success factor for change

The measures of change communication have certain special characteristics. For example, an integrated and repeatedly revised communication plan is a good idea, to ensure that the messages can be consistently coordinated for the respective target groups and their needs. Departmental workshops for the staff entrusted with change communication or – if there is a lack of resources – experienced consultants can be used to help draw up such communication plans.

Important instruments of change communication

There are many instruments and measures that can be used for the internal and external communication of change. However, the cardinal question in this context is often: "How can I use the best and fastest solution for my communication, given the specific change pressure I am under?" An overview containing important methods and measures follows (Table 2). This overview is intended only to provide some general indications on communication methods and the kind of timescales involved in their implementation.

Table 2. Internal measures and means of communication (selection).

Means	Time needed [Speed]	Complexity	Participants [Target group]	Preparation time needed
Telephone	varies [fast]	low	usually 2	none
Intranet	much [fast/instant information]	high, varies according to the subject	intranet team [relatively large, interdepartmental]	several months
Internal survey	medium amount [relatively slow]	low to medium	survey team [depending on scope]	several days
Intranet forums for staff	medium amount [quite fast]	low to medium (depending on subjects)	large [interdepartmental]	several days for installation
Personal communication	varies [fast]	low	1-to-1 communication	none
Integration website	much [fast]	low to high (very flexible in use)	website team [relatively large, interdepartmental]	several months
Push mails	little [fast]	low	1-2 [relatively large]	little
Notice board	little [very topical – if updated]	low	1-2 [relatively large]	little
Telephone conference	little [fast]	low	host + xy [depending on departments involved]	little
Lectures and presentations	quite a lot [relatively slow]	relatively high	1-2 people [usually small]	medium (2-3 weeks)
Workshops	quite a lot [slow due to evaluation]	high	varying [up to several project teams]	relatively high
Fast information services (e.g. newsletter)	little [fast]	low	few [relatively large]	max. ½ day

In addition to specific change communication, the communication of rules should also be accelerated in order to achieve a dynamic and speedy process in the important development phases of the (new) company. Too much information is impossible, and communication can rarely be too fast.

Structural prerequisites for change communication

Certain conditions have to be met within a company if the timing of change communication is to be well-balanced:

- A 'streamlined line of authority' should be established, which, wherever possible, allows immediate decision-making on what information can be passed on and what should not be, in a (pending) merger process. A central Clearing Desk chaired, for example, by a member of the board (Change Champion), as the highest decision-making authority can prove helpful here. The long coordination loops that apply in day-to-day communications in large-scale companies fail miserably in such processes.

- Furthermore, the control of such processes must not be left to chance or detached from the business. Here, as in all other major re-engineering processes, it is essential to define and measure key performance indicators.[2]

- More staff in corporate communications should be engaged who are equipped with enough experience to cope swiftly with the increased workload (on top of the usual day-to-day business). After all, a drastic increase in the frequency of media contacts and events has to be managed during the entire change process. However, this can only succeed if sufficient internal and external (for example, consultants) resources are available.

- Internal communication also provides the basic infrastructure for approaching and talking with external target groups. Customers are very quick to notice when a company speaks with a 'forked tongue'. Field service also contributes towards informing the outside world of the momentary mood within the company. This requires a uniform approach towards orienting and coordinating external and internal communication projects, in order to be able to react quickly. The rule of thumb is to make sure that external announcements are always made at the same time, sending the same basic messages – although they will contain varying amounts of detail and be presented in different ways via different channels.

- Communication with the staff must be emotional. This succeeds best if communication forms are used that promote person-to-person conversations. For this reason, smaller event formats in particular – as well as spontaneous chats in the corridor and the famous "grapevine" – take on a much greater importance during change phases.

Summary: Speed as a basis for change

The frequency and speed of change processes are subject to highly interactive overall conditions that are becoming increasingly global. Change needs top managers who can cope with the external, dynamic processes

---

[2] See the contribution by Rainer Lang and Julia Zangl in this volume.

quickly and flexibly. Management of change is values management and therefore requires professionalism of the highest order in its practical implementation. Changes in products and services, technology, structures and processes in companies and other organisations have become, not only much more frequent with shorter cycles, but simultaneously more complex. Therefore, the only companies that have a future are companies that change successfully and quickly.

Today, the development and promotion of change-management skills in companies has more than ever become a competitive factor that can decide on the success or failure of a transaction.

In the future, the foundation for this must be provided by excellently trained communication specialists, without whom there can be no change to patterns that are geared to dynamically changing market situations. This means, in particular, that change can no longer be practised sustainably today without communication that repeatedly proves itself to be flexible. The crucial prerequisite is that the speed of change must be geared to the target groups according to the three Ps (Portfolio, Process, People) and must be continuously reviewed; otherwise many promising change projects – even ones with excellent economic prospects – will be doomed to failure from the outset. In these cases, change communication will have to be replaced by crisis communication.

The power of ideas – Reputation management and successful change

Robert Wreschniok

"Everything we do begins with an idea"
David Lynch 2007

Historical and political transformation research shows that societal upheavals – such as the development of nation states at the beginning of the Enlightenment or the transformation of the political, economic and societal systems in Eastern Europe after the Cold War – were given decisive momentum by the respectively dominant idea systems, e.g. the nation state, democracy and human rights. The inspiration for these mega-transformations, which caused profound changes in all areas of life for millions of people, came from a surprisingly small number of people who moulded and asserted the idea systems of their times by dint of their position in society and in opinion-forming environments. This contribution examines what conclusions can be drawn from this observation for corporate change processes and what role can be played in this context by active reputation management. A concrete example from the financial sector will be given to show how the observance of the laws of modern reputation management can become the key to successful change management.

The discussion on how nation states actually came to being is still clogged with legends. 19th century historians gave preference to the theory of an evolutionary development: the nation was seen as an organically growing, homogeneous and timeless cultural community which is constituted naturally by territory and people (Smith 1998). In the course of time, a national feeling emerges and grows among the tribes, nourished by their desire to set up their own state in which to practise their own culture.

For about the last two decades, modern nationalism research has been radically questioning such traditional ideas. Putting this sweeping change of perspective in a nutshell, James Donald, a renowned researcher on nationalism, says: "It was not the nation that generated nationalism; rather, the idea system of nationalism created its nation" (James 1995). Or to put it more succinctly: "People make nations" (Gellner 1991). In other words, in the 18th century it was a fascinating idea that made the concept of the nation the dominating political force right up to the present day – not only in Germany, but also in many other parts of the world. And, of course, it was people, strictly speaking a relatively small number of opinion leaders, who were behind this idea. Today, historians (in Germany, for example) speak of a few hundred, some of only a handful of professors, theologians, writers, students and high-school students who significantly shaped and asserted the idea system of the nation and helped develop it into what it is today (Der Spiegel 2007). Thus, a small number of people decisively changed the lives of millions and caused a profound change in the societal, political and economic system.[1]

This brief digression into a controversial historical debate on the development of the nation state opens up interesting issues for corporate change management:

1. What role is played by idea systems and their assertion in corporate change processes? And what strategies and methods can be used to apply this to change management?
2. If a few hundred people are enough to form a nation out of millions, how few participants is a company likely to need to organise real change? And what kind of people are they? How can they be found and deployed to help direct change?

The following paper seeks an answer to these questions by discussing what function the striving for "reputation" has in the development and dissemination of idea systems in our society, and what role is attributed to "reputation bearers" in social, political − and specifically – economic change processes.

---

[1] That this is not a singular historical phenomenon is shown by comparable development processes, e.g. the emergence and global spread of capitalism and communism, the idea of liberalism and growing interdependence, i.e. the economic networking primarily of the "Western" nation states and, of course, the no-longer-so-new mega idea system of "globalization". Beginning in the 18th and continuing into the 21st century, key importance for the transformation of the societal, political and economic systems is attributed to idea systems – or ideologies, to use a more negative term. The key assertion is that the credit for social cohesion essentially goes to communicative structures (Deutsch 1966).

Reputation, an acquirable good

If you can explain how trust/reputation develops and disintegrates in institutions, organizations and people, you have the crucial point for explaining social action and social policy (Eisenegger 2005).

In the historical epoch of the Enlightenment (Imhof and Romano 1996) (which partially coincides with the example referred to above of the slowly successful idea of the nation) the "aristocracy of education" began to successively replace the "aristocracy of birth" (Imhof and Romano 1996). This refers to a process that transformed the closed, quasi-feudal society, in which the rank and reputation of its members was determined by their origin, into today's pluralistic and open media society where, in principle, every individual has a chance to achieve a position in society, business or politics.

The transformation of the social function of honour is closely connected with this development. In the pre-modern feudal society, if someone questioned your social position, this was regarded as an insult to your honour. Honour, as a pre-modern form of recognition, was historically replaced by reputation as a specifically modern form of recognition. Today, reputation has become an acquirable good (Voswinkel 1999). It legitimises the societal position of people in science, business (Schwallbach 2002, Schweiger 2003) and politics. Furthermore, reputation has simultaneously become a fragile good in the process of freeing itself in the modern media society from quasi-feudal references to birth and developing from a collective concept (allocation of honour in feudal society) into an individual concept (allocation of reputation to people or institutions). The reputation of people in leading positions in business, politics or science – as well as the reputation of companies or institutions – is produced by communication. In the media society, there is permanent suspicion that it is all just show.

Reputation therefore has a key function in change processes. It is reputation bearers that head-hunters are looking for; they are the ones who are appointed as corporate executives and accepted as trustworthy. Reputation bearers legitimise ideas and strategies and can see them through. They are the key success factor when directing corporate change processes – because they achieve the necessary degree of acceptance for the idea and the associated aims of change. And it seems a logical conclusion that strategies and management methods that take this into account will be particularly successful in change processes.

The circumstance that reputation is produced by communication in this context gives communication management a key role in change processes. This circumstance also offers an answer to the question posed at the outset, i.e. how many players are needed to organise real change in a company. In the final analysis, only a few reputation bearers are needed to legitimise the need for a change or the chance of a change for many people.

For reputation can be strategically exchanged for trust. People have a tendency to trust reputation bearers; "advance trust" is a commonly used phrase in this context. Therefore, when change is defined and organisational aims are proclaimed, a leadership function falls to reputation bearers, e.g. a company's CEO. The CEO lays down the guiding principle of the change and legitimises this idea on the strength of his own reputation as the company's helmsman. And it becomes evident what elementary problems loom for a change project if the laws and regularities that determine the emergence or loss of reputation – or trust in the management personnel or the company – are ignored in the attendant communication.

Reputation management in change processes: Laws and regulations

Active reputation management in change processes focuses on three levers:

1. Business reputation: this requires competent compliance with functional role requirements (competence), which is enforced primarily by CEOs and their top management.[2]
2. Social reputation: this requires the observance of socio-moral standards (integrity), e.g. measured by the decisions taken by management for target achievement in the context of a change project. Change management must do justice to the expectations of the executives and staff affected by the planned change in terms of socially responsible behaviour in order to legitimise their positions of status and power – usually by communication – and thus secure their "licence to operate" in the change process (Hansen 2000).
3. Reputation identity: this highlights the individual and emotionally binding aspect. In change projects, what was described in the introductory example as national feeling is frequently called "necessary authenticity" or the "we feeling".

In the course of the last decade, intensive research in the field of reputation management (Eisenegger and Imhof 2004) has identified certain regulari-

---

[2] A number of recent studies show how crucial the role of the CEO is in change processes. See among others Smythe 2005, p. 14.

ties and laws in handling these three levers; observing them gives the people responsible for communications an astonishing amount of creative scope in phases during which reputation either is produced or declines. 'Astonishing' because the empirical studies have led to a number of real paradigm changes for strategic communication management. Here are three examples. It has been empirically shown that if a company's or an executive's social reputation is too good, this is harmful for their overall reputation. Furthermore, it has been proven in the meantime that an excessive degree of personalisation in internal or external communications, e.g. on the part of CEOs, can pose a real reputation risk. And it is wishful thinking to believe that a high level of response (e.g. measured in the number of press clippings) is synonymous with a value contribution for the company. The opposite is the case. Studies in the field of reputation research have shown that high or excessive response values in particular can become a risk for reputation performance. These three examples alone show that communication management is a lot more scientific with the methods available today; figuratively speaking, one might say it has made the transition from, say, natural healing to mainstream medicine. The following example from the financial sector shows how the value contribution from communications in change processes can be noticeably increased by observing the regularities of reputation management.

An example from the financial sector

In 2007, a leading and already very profitable German wealth manager had very ambitious growth targets. In order to achieve them, the management board approved the implementation of an excellence programme with five modules (corresponding to the five business areas) and a total of 20 subprojects (four projects per module aimed at ensuring target achievement). The programme was launched in March 2007 and is scheduled to run until the end of 2008. Although its objectives had been explained to all the employees in target agreements concluded in one-to-one staff meetings, held both at the central office and in the sales department, there were considerable misgivings that the "programme from the central office" would ultimately not be implemented actively by all employees in all the 20 branch offices and 48 locations. These worries led to the key question as to how the company could muster the necessary support and active participation in the central office and particularly the regionally organised sales department under extreme pressure (shortage of time, possible resistance, and limited resources).

It was clear from the outset that communication would have a dual function here: first, to develop a classic communication programme to inform the staff about the excellence programme by means of clearly structured information (initial situation, objectives, responsibilities) and second, to launch a reputation-management process that would mobilise the staff, encourage them to become active supporters of the programme's objectives, and also help direct the change process.

The communication programme: Accompanying change

It was clear that, in a traditional bank, the staff would have certain expectations regarding communication. A conservative programme, i.e. classic cascade communication, was therefore deliberately used. Accordingly, the staff were informed about the excellence programme in a letter from the management board. Managers explained the details at the local weekly team meetings, and a special newsletter commented on the programme's progress for the first few weeks. Parallel to the dispatch of the first newsletter, a website was launched in the intranet for use as an information platform on all aspects of the individual projects. The key challenge for communication lay in structuring the very complex excellence programme, developing the didactics, explaining the programme clearly and understandably in simple messages, and processing it visually (logo, uniform design of communication instruments) in such a way as to encourage the staff to identify with the programme.

The reputation-management process: Directing change

In order to ensure the manageability of the change process with increasing staff participation, the mobilisation programme used the logic of reputation management as a source of orientation. Whereas communication initially concentrated on logically relating the complex contents of the 20 sub-projects to the company's business objectives, the focus was now on issues relating to the central, guiding principle and who was to get this principle across. In the same way that nationalism created its own nation and led to profound changes in human behaviour, the aim now was to establish an idea system that was to create, on a meta-level, the framework for the future staff behaviour that would be necessary for target achievement. This guiding principle was developed and officially adopted in several workshops. It became clear that all employees had to become aware of their individual responsibility for the success of the excellence programme and that the only way to achieve the desired improvements – i.e. lower costs, time savings and productivity increases in the company – was by personal initiative and active participation. Following up this realisation, it was agreed that the guiding principle should be entrepreneurship – or the establishment of an *intra*-preneurial spirit – among the wealth manager's staff. The aim of the accompanying reputation management process was thus to lay the foundations on which the staff would be able to work creatively "like an entrepreneur in the company" and make a major value contribution to their own company by their own personal initiative and participation.

The development of the guiding principle of a new entrepreneurial spirit was prepared in several phases, taking into account the reputation regularities referred to above. The first step was to transform the communication programme described above step-by-step from a top-down system into a bottom-up approach. This was extremely important for the acceptance of the entire programme during the establishment phase. Hence, the intensity of communication was deliberately reduced at the end of the establishment phase. At the same time, the degree of personalisation with the CEO was markedly cut back after he had performed his legitimisation function for the excellence programme as the highest reputation bearer by demonstrating a great deal of management attention. The delegation of responsibility from the CEO to his staff – i.e. the transition from a concept based on following instructions to one focusing on the staff's personal responsibility in the excellence programme – was underlined by a targeted development of the CEO's social reputation and by reducing focus on the attributes relating to his business reputation (Kaplan and Norton 2004). The main subjects of communication switched from facts and figures, yield targets and the management programme to aspects aimed at promoting trust and to the key role of staff. The decisive success factor for the implementation of the idea system of entrepreneurship and *intra*-preneurial spirit, however, was the appointment of 20 carefully selected reputation bearers at the bank. As part of the so-called Excellence Agents Programme, the CEO (symbolically) handed over responsibility for the success of the excellence programme to selected members of staff. In the places where contact between the module managers responsible for sub-projects at central office on the one hand and sales staff in the regions on the other were maintained by means of newsletters and letters from the managing board 20 reputation bearers were also carefully chosen from among the staff and entrusted with these managerial tasks in a constituent meeting at the company's central office.

Selection process and nomination of the excellence agents

It was clear from the outset that excellence agents would have to be in a position of trust among staff with regard to their competence and integrity (business and social reputation) if they were to have a positive influence on their colleagues and persuade them to take part in the programme and the active shaping of the excellence process. The excellence agents were therefore not selected by means of a "grass-roots democratic" process (for example, by applying to become an excellence agent), but were instead appointed by the management board in close coordination with the branch-office managers responsible for personnel in the regions. The defined profile of the agents corresponded to the model of the "entrepreneur in the company": they had to be regarded at their locations as role models – in terms of both their business performance and their attitude to work (showing personal initiative) – and simultaneously enjoy the support of the employees at their location and personify a true *intra*-preneurial spirit by means of their social behaviour and communicative skills. The excellence agents were described by those involved as people who are very well informed and credible at the same time. They were role models in the opinion-forming process among colleagues. Their intense interaction with direct superiors – and, in the context of the process, with selected managers in higher executive positions right up to the CEO – helped legitimise the content that the excellence agents extracted from the conventional cascade communication system and spread horizontally among their colleagues. Within the company, the excellence agents took on precisely the function that the reputation bearers had performed in the socio-political and economic transformation processes during the formation of nation states, as referred to earlier, both at the communication level just mentioned and at the social level. At the social level, the excellence agents convinced their colleagues, thanks to their technical expertise, their business success, a high measure of practised integrity and their open-mindedness towards innovations and changes.

They were invited to join this small circle by a letter from the CEO, underlining his personal appreciation and the importance of the task. All the agents without exception agreed to take on the function.

Leading the change

From that point on, the idea was for the excellence agents to encourage and document the increasing participation of the staff. In the course of communication, an overview of all agents was published with their contact details and areas of responsibility. In the fourth calendar week of the excellence programme, all employees were informed about the excellence agents, their role, tasks and objectives, and were asked to do their best to support the agents in their work. Once the agents had started working, the staff were able to get involved in the programme directly. A feedback function to all subprojects of the programme and a reward system for active participation were also available.

A special "film script" was developed to direct the work of the excellence agents over a period of several months. In weekly mission briefings, the agents were centrally directed according to the principle of "leading by objectives". This *intra*-preneurial principle was the model for the entire programme. From this time on, the excellence agents supported the entire excellence process as ambassadors in the branch offices and acted at the same time as spokespersons for the staff. The agents more than did justice to their three functions, i.e. to inform, motivate and activate. With a participation ratio of over 86 percent of all employees in the sales department and central office, the set objectives were exceeded after less than six weeks, thanks to the efforts of the excellence agents.

The excellence agent programme culminated in a central staff meeting. Over a weekend, all staff members were informed in detail about the intermediate results and milestones of the excellence programme. In a total of 48 workshops, all employees and managers including the management board and general managers compiled – on the basis of the 20 projects developed in the excellence programme – concrete task packages and action programmes to be completed by the end of the year on the personal initiative of the individual sales teams all over Germany. On this occasion, the new self-image of being an "entrepreneur in your own company" became tangible for the first time. On the second day of the staff meeting, the new *intra*-preneurial spirit was further encouraged by a comprehensive programme aimed at strengthening group dynamics and consolidating each person's individual sense of entrepreneurship. The spontaneous feedback and a detailed written survey of all staff after the meeting showed that the first phase of the excellence programme had been successfully completed. All the results now indicate that a new form of entrepreneurial thinking is becoming established among the employees at the central office and in the sales department.

Outlook

The coming months and years will show whether the company has managed to establish the idea of the *intra*-preneurial spirit among the staff. Encouraged by the successes, the programme has now been further fine-tuned in-line with the underlying communications strategy. The focus is no

longer on describing the individual excellence projects and intensely famil-
iarising the staff with the projects, but on completing and implementing
the task packages and action programmes jointly drawn up in the workshops. For this purpose, concrete examples of best practice by staff in the
individual regions will be collected by the excellence agents in the near future and made accessible to all staff. The staff can now choose for themselves which of the 20 different approaches they would like to pursue – either alone or in a team – in order to achieve the set objectives by the end of
the year.

Conclusion

And indeed economic and biological competition would proceed according to
the same pattern of gradual evolutionary development if it were not for the corporate strategy: it [can] accelerate the effects of competition and the pace of change
[...]. Strategic competition thus has a very decisive effect: it speeds things up (Oetinger 1998).

This paper began by stating that it was not the nation that created nationalism, but the idea system of nationalism that created the nation. Only a
handful of professors, theologians, writers, students and high-school students were needed to do this, and they decisively influenced and implemented the idea of the nation – until it evolved to the stage of development
we see today. Research into the laws and regularities of reputation development in recent years has succeeded in unravelling some of the forces
that shape this phenomenon, i.e. societal change caused by a small number
of players. The example of a change process in a financial company was
used to show how these insights can be applied to communication and
change management in order to greatly increase the efficiency and success
prospects of such processes. Taking up the initial "historical" assertion, as
it were, a small team of excellence agents – carefully selected reputation
bearers from among the staff – were transformed into an engine of change.
Integrated into a comprehensive communication programme geared towards the rules of reputation management (paying attention to the relative
importance of business and social reputation and the degree of personalisation and response), they achieved an unusually high participation ratio and
a profound change of consciousness, and this has prepared the ground for
more and fresh *intra*-preneurial spirit among the staff – all in an unusually
short time. It was shown that a dual communication function led to this
success: namely, although the change process was accompanied by conventional communication, it was at the same time actively directed by a

reputation management programme. The approach described also showed that it was not a single new instrument, or a creative flash of inspiration – let alone a revolutionary technology – that achieved this success, but the courage to abandon old ideas and leave well-trodden paths. This is where the key to successful change management lies – in seizing the opportunities that modern reputation management offers to those responsible for communications.

References

Deutsch, Karl (1966) Nationalism and Social Communication. In: Hutchinson, John/Smith, Anthony D. (eds) (1994) Nationalism. Oxford University Press, Oxford/New York, pp 26–29

Eisenegger, Mark (2005) Reputation in der Mediengesellschaft. Konstitution – Issues Monitoring – Issues Management (in German). VS Verlag für Sozialwissenschaften, Wiesbaden

Eisenegger, Mark (2003) Reputationskonstitution in der Mediengesellschaft (in German). In: Jarren, Otfried/Imhof, Kurt/Blum, Toger (eds) Mediengesellschaft, Opladen

Eisenegger, Mark/Imhof, Kurt (2004) Reputationsrisiken moderner Organisationen (in German). In: Ulrike Röttger (ed) Theorien der Public Relations. VS Verlag für Sozialwissenschaften, Wiesbaden, pp 235–256

Hansen, J. (2000) Professionelles Investor Relations Management (in German). Landsberg Lech

Higson, Andrew (1995) Waving the flag. Constructing a National Cinema in Britain. Clarendon Press, Oxford

Imhof, Kurt/Gaetano, Romano (1996) Die Diskontinuität der Moderne. Zur Theorie des sozialen Wandels (in German). Frankfurt/New York, pp 68–129

Kaplan, R.S./Norton, D.P. (2004) Immaterielle Werte – Grünes Licht für Ihre Strategie (in German). Harvard Business Manager, 26. Vol. 5: 18–33

Oetinger, Bolko von (1998) Das Boston Consulting Group Strategie-Buch. Die wichtigsten Managementkonzepte für den Praktiker (in German). Duesseldorf

Schwaiger, Manfred/Hupp, Oliver (2003) Corporate Reputation Management – Herausforderung für die Zukunft (in German). Planung & Analyse, 3/2003b: 58–64

Schwalbach, Joachim (2002) Unternehmensreputation als Erfolgsfaktor (in German). In: Reese/Söllner/Utzig (eds) Relationship Marketing. Standortbestimmung und Perspektiven. Berlin, pp 225–238

Smith, A.D. (1998) Nationalism and Modernity. Routledge, London/New York

Smythe, John (2005) Engaging Employees: How To Create a Communication Culture That Delivers. London

Voswinkel, Stephan (1999) Anerkennung und Reputation. Die Dramaturgie indus-
    trieller Beziehungen. Mit einer Fallstudie zum Bündnis für Arbeit (in Ger-
    man). Konstanz, pp 12
Wiedmann, Klaus-Peter/Buxel, Holger (2004) Reputationsmanagement. Stellen-
    wert und Umsetzung in deutschen Unternehmen – empirische Ergebnisse und
    kritische Einschätzung (in German). PR Magazin 8/2004: 51–58

Change management in alliances

Theresia Theurl and Eric Meyer

Change management usually refers to a change within a company. This is increasingly inappropriate since more and more companies are working together with partners in alliances, joint ventures or other cooperative arrangements. Therefore, appropriate tools have to be developed to manage change in alliances. This contribution shows how suitable construction and management of alliances may facilitate change and what specifics have to be considered in the change management of alliances.

As companies focus on their core competencies, an increasing part of their activities are completed together with partners in some kind of cooperative arrangement.[1] A common trait of cooperations is that there is no direct control on the partner's activities. They cannot be completely monitored, nor can they be immediately influenced. But a partner's activities, i.e. their products, services or the information they generate, significantly contribute to a company's value added. Therefore, the boundaries of the firm are becoming less and less clear-cut. Companies rely heavily on the activities of their partners, which are out of their control or which they have at most limited influence over. We observe numerous examples of such cooperative arrangements: the Star Alliance, a cooperation of airlines, the collaboration of hardware and software producers in computer industry (e.g. Microsoft and AMD), or the supply chain partnerships in the automotive industry (for example, the case of BMW and Magna Steyr producing BMW's X3), to name but a few.

---

[1] Due to lack of space we will not distinguish the different types of cooperative arrangements like strategic alliances, joint ventures or contractual agreements, although the type of arrangement has a significant influence on the change management. (The effects can be easily derived from the general conclusions we present.) Therefore, we use the terms "cooperation" and "alliance" synonymously.

Traditional management techniques relying on command and control are inapt for this new environment. On the other hand, companies reap the benefits of economies of scale and enhance their flexibility by employing the know-how and competitive advantages of their partners. Thus, managing the boundaries of the firm has become a major task for senior management.

Unfortunately, this has not been recognised by many senior managers. Consequently, cooperative arrangements like strategic alliances or partner agreements are not integrated into a holistic partner concept. It is virtually unknown what value the partners contribute to the firm's output, and many senior managers simply apply the same management techniques used in their company to the management of their alliances. This results in inferior returns that do not meet the management's expectations.

Building and managing alliances

Using alliances as an organisational device immediately implies a certain degree of flexibility and therefore of change. Consequently, constructing and managing an alliance gains much more importance for change management than in ordinary cases in a company, since this continuous process of change depends on the alliance being solidly constructed. Insufficient construction or management will therefore lead to severe backlash on the ability to change and on the change management of an alliance. To put it clearly: a well-constructed alliance will have no need for separate change management since change is an inherent part of the alliance's management. Needless to say, this ideal rarely applies.

The process of building and managing alliances can be subdivided into five consecutive steps (Fig. 1).[2]

Step 1: Strategic positioning

This is perhaps the most important and most underestimated step. The company has to analyse its value chain and slice it into many little steps, which creates a sort of map of the company's value network. It has to decide on its strengths (management speak: core competencies) and on those parts of the value chain that are only of minor relevance for the company or that are beyond its capabilities. For every interface between two steps of the value chain, the management has to identify which products, which

---

[2] For a more detailed description of the process of cooperation, see Theurl 2005, p 173.

services and which information is transferred. The purpose is to find out those parts of the value chain that might be handed over to partners and how these parts of the processes, that are given away, feed into the parts of the value chain that remain within the company. Evidently, this is essential for future change management, since it lays down the basis for analysing the impact of changes. If a company is not aware of the relations to its partners, it will have substantial problems in, first, identifying the impact of change on its partners and, second, communicating this change to the partner.

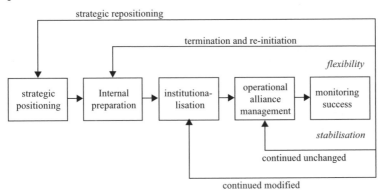

Fig. 1. The process of cooperation

Step 2: Internal preparation

After the decision has been made on the parts of the value chain that are to be produced by partners or together with partners, the internal preparation starts. Since cooperative processes cannot be managed by the same instruments as internal processes, cooperation competence has to be allocated in the management (preferably in the senior management). Moreover, the interfaces to the potential partners have to be prepared. Each company needs to substantiate its own requirements for production, for example, what information is necessary for production, which quality standards are required, etc. Many computer producers cooperate with certified partners to service their hardware. Obviously, these partners generate a lot of information on the hardware's reliability and malfunctions as well as on customer demands. It has to be certain that this information is fed back, even though it does not originate from the hardware producing company.

Finally, partners must be screened. There are many tools helping companies identify the right partners. Basically, there are three dimensions:

1. Strategic fit: Is the partner pursuing a similar strategy as the company seeking a partner (e.g. quality leader)?
2. Operational fit: Does the partner provide the products to the required quality? Is the partner able to implement the procedures that are necessary for the management of the cooperation?
3. Cultural fit: Does the partner adhere to a similar management culture? In particular: Is the partner able to implement a collaborative management style that emphasises a more coordinating approach rather than top-down "command and control" techniques?

Step 3: Institutionalisation

The institutionalisation is pivotal for the cooperation, as well as for the change management, that may be necessary. It fixes the complete 'infrastructure' of the cooperation between the partners. The partners agree on:

- their cooperation targets
- the type of cooperation (loose contractual agreement, strategic alliance, joint venture, franchising, etc.)
- pricing of products and services
- rules (including exit rules)
- communication standards

Although all of these decisions are important, it is worth considering the last two of them more closely. Cooperative arrangements are assumed to make production more flexible and therefore to facilitate change. This effect is predominantly driven by the decision on the rules of cooperation. The cooperating partners abandon their control over the partner's part of the value chain but agree on certain rules of their cooperation, i.e. the partners are free to operate as long as they obey the agreed rules. Depending on the strictness of the rules, the partners are more or less free to change their production if environmental conditions change. Thus, the partner will not get involved in this change as long as the rules and the provided goods, services or information remain untouched. If the rules or the supplied goods, services or information are affected, the communication standards come into play. Cooperation does not work by the usual "command and control" management techniques.[3] Rather, communicative and collaborative skills are required for successfully managing cooperative arrangements. Therefore, starting a cooperation means determining clear-cut communication paths and information standards. This is beneficial for

---

[3] Malone (2004) describes this move from "command and control" to "coordinate and cultivate".

governing the cooperation (see Step 4) as well as in situations of change where rules might have to be modified.

Step 4: Operational alliance management

After the cooperation has started, the main task is to govern the relationships with the partners. This essentially refers to the monitoring of the interfaces to the partners, which will guarantee the integration of the cooperation to the company's own production processes.

Step 5: Monitoring success

In the final step, the cooperation's success has to be monitored, evaluated and compared to the targets defined at the outset of the cooperation. Monitoring is of course an ongoing task that accompanies the operation of any alliance. The evaluation process results will suggest different measures to improve the cooperation's performance.

The benchmark case: Continuous change

As mentioned above, change is inherent to the management of an alliance. This final evaluation step feeds back into the prior steps and designates different intensities of change (see Fig. 1).

The evaluation process is the starting point for cooperative change management. If the targets are reached, then nothing must be changed and the cooperation continues unchanged.

If the targets are not reached, the causes for this failure have to be analysed. In many cases, this under-performance, especially at the beginning of a cooperation, is due to insufficiencies in the 'infrastructure': some rules might turn out to be inappropriate, the communication between the partners might not work as originally conceived or the supplied goods may lack the required quality. These problems can usually be tackled by adapting the institutionalisation of the cooperation, which may also imply altering the intensity of the cooperation. In some cases, this will lead to integrative solutions, i.e. the acquisition of the partner.

If changes of the institutionalisation do not accomplish the desired results, but a cooperation still seems to be indicated, then a termination of the cooperation with this special partner and the re-initiation of the cooperation with another partner may be advisable. In this case the internal preparation of Step 2 has to be restarted.

Finally, if there is a strategic repositioning that significantly alters the company's value chain (maybe due to environmental changes), then the process returns to Step 1 and again starts with a new strategic positioning. This can imply that the existing cooperation will cease.

In summary, cooperative arrangements are by themselves more flexible and better suited for change, as long as they are appropriately constructed, i.e. as long as the necessary feedback mechanisms are part of the cooperating partners' idea of cooperation. However, in reality, alliances nevertheless need some kind of change management in order to implement the above mentioned changes.

Change management in alliances – Considering the specifics

Success in change management processes has been greatly considered in management research.[4] For closer insight, we refer the reader to the other contributions in this volume. As a short reminder, the four basic success factors are:

1. Communication of the relevance of change
2. A clear (joint) vision for the future
3. Communication to the employees/stakeholders
4. A clear commitment to change

These factors also apply to change management in alliances. But their implementation is made more difficult.

Maybe the most important obstacle to change in alliances is inertia, which stems from different sources.[5] As we will see by examining the causes for this inertia, well-constructed alliances with appropriate communication and responsibility structures are much less jeopardised by inertia.

Less well constructed alliances are always subject to this problem of inertia. Although cooperations are frequently constructed to enter new markets and therefore should be able to quickly adapt to new environments or new experiences that have been gained in these markets, they can exhibit a surprising inability to change. But while this inertia within a company can

---

[4] See, for example, the eight-stage process of change management by Kotter (1995) and Kotter (1996), the DICE-method by Sirkin, Keenan and Jackson (2005) or the textbook description by Johnson, Scholes and Whittington (2005), p 503.

[5] For a closer examination of inertia in alliances see for example Ernst and Bramford (2005), p 139.

usually be attributed to a fear of the new, the reasons in a cooperation are vastly different. The three main reasons for inertia that have to be tackled are: communication, competence and contract.

How to overcome the communication problem

The relevance of change is harder to communicate between companies than within companies, since the communication paths between the cooperation partners are not yet established. Therefore, the urgency for change cannot be communicated quickly enough to the right people in the management of the partner company.

Two cases should be distinguished. First, there is the case where the change concerns the fundamentals of the cooperation. In a poorly conceived cooperation, the evaluation of the cooperation is insufficient or the partners have different evaluation methods, leading to different results that disguise the urgency for change. Second, there is the case where the need for change stems from within the company but also affects the cooperation and therefore the partner involved in this cooperation. This is an even harder challenge.

Communicating the need for change requires the explanation to the partner that the company's current returns are unsatisfactory and therefore require change. For the partner company three problems arise:

1. It is unsure how reliable the information is, thus it cannot estimate how urgent change is.
2. Even if it deems the information reliable, it is still unsure how successful the change management of the company will be. An inconclusive change could also seriously affect the partner company's business.
3. Business with this company is not the partner company's only business. Thus, the impact on the partner company's business may be smaller, hence reducing the perceived urgency for change.

Overcoming these communication problems in a change management process boils down to a fast-track implementation of the cooperation process.

First, not recognising the urgency of change is due to a lack of understanding the joint value chain. Companies usually deem themselves more independent than they actually are. Therefore awareness of the partners' interdependence has to be increased. The only way to achieve this joint understanding is to swiftly agree on meetings of the 'right' people.[6] These people are characterised by a deep knowledge of each companies' value chain, so they can quickly estimate the relevance of the partner for their own production and the impact of the proposed change.

Second, overcoming the problems in identifying the partner's competence to implement change can be solved by signalling and screening devices. The change-invoking partner could signal their commitment by investing in the change process and explaining the company's vision. An appropriate screening device could be an invitation to the partner company. It has proven to be extremely useful to set up small teams consisting of one or two mid-management employees to visit the other company in recognition of the need for change and the possibility for change.[7]

Third, the 'minority' problem is very hard to overcome. If the alliance has only a minor contribution to the value added, the inclination to invest in change will be quite low. Thus, the only way to tackle this problem is either to finance the required change in the partner company or to exit the alliance.

How to overcome the competence problem

The people in the partner company receive the information that change is needed, but are not able to handle this information correctly for different reasons:

- They do not have the competence to act on this issue and have to hand over the information to someone who is responsible for change in the partner company.
- They do not have the professional competence and thus are unable to derive either the right measures within the company or the right measures for change for the cooperation.
- Managing the cooperation is just an additional occupation of a manager and the work on the cooperation is deferred indefinitely.

The competence problem is clearly a management problem caused by inadequate design of the alliance. Curing these inadequacies is a rather tedious and time-consuming task. Tackling the problem calls for a two-step meeting approach. In a first meeting, the requirements for change are dis-

---

[6] The 'right' people problem is tackled below.

[7] In manufacturing alliances such small teams are very common. Besides the yield of a common understanding of production, it also helps to reap the benefits of a learning curve.

cussed and the necessary decisions for this change are derived. Each participant returns to their company in order to create a responsibility map, i.e. a map clearly indicating decision-making responsibilities within a company, which will facilitate and accelerate the change process. In a second meeting, relevant decision makers are invited to discuss the necessity of change. In this meeting, the need for an appropriate communication will re-emerge (see the item above). Evidently, the creation of an alliance responsibility in a company would be an ideal solution, but is rather unlikely in a change process.

The role of contracts

The negotiations on the contract or on some of the rules may have been very difficult. In such cases, the partners will be reluctant to change, since that would involve a costly renegotiating of these issues in the contract. It is in the nature of a contract that there is no immediate ex-post remedy for this problem. The only way to overcome this problem is to include the change process in the contract by introducing conflict resolution mechanisms and exit solutions.

Conclusion

Cooperation is a way to gain flexibility and therefore to facilitate change in response to external shocks. But these gains do not come for free. It is necessary to analyse whether a cooperation is the best organisational solution and then to design the cooperation properly. The main points that have to be implemented in order to make change in a cooperation easier are:

- designing a partner management scheme that help to identify important partners
- devising (joint) evaluation schemes for the success of the cooperation
- assigning competencies for managers managing the cooperation
- implementing communication ways between the partners.

References

Ernst, David/Bamford, James (2005) Your Alliances Are Too Stable. In: Harvard Business Review, Vol. 83, Issue 6 (June): 133–141

Johnson, Gerry/Scholes, Kevan/Whittington, Richard (2005) Exploring Corporate Strategy. Harlow et al., Pearson

Kotter, John P. (1995) Leading Change – Why Transformation efforts fail. In: Harvard Business Review, Vol. 73, Issue 2 (March/April): 59–67

Kotter, John P. (1996) Leading Change. Harvard Business School Press, Boston

Malone, Thomas (2004) The future of work. Harvard Business School Press, Boston

Sirkin, Harold L./Keenan, Perry/Jackson, Alan (2005) The hard side of change management. In: Harvard Business Review, Vol. 83, Issue 10: 108–118

Theurl, Theresia (2005) From Corporate to Cooperative Governance. In: Theurl, Theresia (ed) Economics of Interfirm Networks. Mohr Siebeck, Tuebingen, pp 149–192

Insight

The world is changing very fast. Big will not beat small anymore. It will be the fast beating the slow.

Rupert Murdoch, CEO News Corporation, 1979–present

Winning people's hearts and minds

Katrin Schwabe

During organisational change the foremost task of communication is to guide all people involved through the different stages of the process. Therefore, it must go beyond the plain provision of information and messaging, in order to ensure understanding and create commitment. But this is where most change communication fails, and there are many reasons for this: time constraints, limited resources, lack of management involvement, absence of stimuli for interaction and inapt use of media – to name a few. One effective approach to successful change communication is to create dialogue and engagement within and across organisational levels and borders. In doing so – and with the support of a result-oriented measurement process – it becomes a powerful vehicle for building trust, which is the most important resource for ensuring change takes place and is long-lasting.

Change communication has to deal with ever-shortening cycles that are usually accompanied by pressure on time and finances. Against this background, organisations may decide to invest more money in new technology and big events – following the maxim 'bigger and louder'. But, as people say, bigger is not always better! A much more effective lever for change communication is to open it up and generate and facilitate dialogue on specific issues and learn from it.

The power of dialogue

Dialogue as a change communication tool is not about creating an arbitrary feedback loop from employees to management. It is about having a conversation that provides space for exploration and reflection of content and messages delivered to an audience. In this context, dialogue addresses a multitude of obstacles that frequently hinder successful change implementation, as it

- considers different perspectives and expertise allowing complexity to be explored from different angles
- clarifies the assumptions under which a choice for change has been made
- answers questions and acts as a catalyst for new ones
- deepens the understanding of why change is necessary
- provides a glimpse into the future – in order to share excitement, concerns and potential benefits
- explains how the change will affect the individual

Furthermore, dialogue guides each individual through a learning curve. Any facilitator of change dialogue is challenged with being open-minded, listening to concerns and arguing credibly and honestly in order to steer a relevant and fruitful conversation. Making managers across all levels responsible for facilitating change dialogues, ensures they are forced to walk the talk. Dialogue bridges the critical gap between 'Do as I say' and 'Do as I do'. It puts the key players in the front line.

By nature, dialogue carries the risk of getting out of hand and turning into a session of blaming and finger-pointing. If that is the case, the image of an organisation's leadership capability is at stake. Successful and constructive dialogue requires structure, preparation and practice. But which tool is the right one to choose?

Tools for successful dialogue

A number of effective dialogue formats are available, each fulfilling a specific purpose along the change journey. One of the most essential factors for success, that dialogue can support, is reaching many people within a short timeframe whilst providing an individual experience for the audience.

Cascading waves – 'Time to people'

Speed is critical in change communication. Organisations can't afford to take months to communicate a new strategy to all their employees. The concept of cascading waves is a very efficient approach to reaching out to many in a short time frame. Each wave of dialogue sessions covers one to two organisational levels. Managers of the level above act as facilitators. The current participants of dialogue sessions are then selected for facilitating the next wave down in the organisation.

As the proportion of dialogue participants usually increases with each level, the amount of facilitators needs to be increased accordingly. For every 500 participants, a pool of about five or six facilitators is useful. With an average session size of 20–30 participants, each facilitator has to conduct about five sessions. In terms of time, if the dialogues are short enough to be incorporated into existing team meetings, an organisation can reach 10,000 employees within three to four months. If additional meetings need to take place, it will take about six months to reach the same number of people. The disadvantage of using existing meetings is that the dialogue topic is considered as an integral part of the operational business. It makes the subject appear less important. By contrast, creating a special meeting space has the advantage of making the dialogue stick out from all other communication.

The dialogue content that is cascaded should not vary significantly between organisational levels for two reasons:

1. Consistency of messages is a critical success factor for communicating change from top to bottom, otherwise rumours, anxiety, confusion and frustration can quickly surface.
2. The more alike the dialogue is, the easier its deployment on the next level becomes.

Good preparation by the facilitators is crucial for conducting successful dialogue. Train-the-trainer sessions enable future facilitators to practice leading the dialogue and increase their confidence in the content due to be discussed. In addition to this live preparation, it is recommended that download platforms are set up to give access to relevant support tools, such as facilitation guides, presentation templates, preparation checklists, case studies and role-play scenarios.

Town hall meetings – Keeping stakeholders in the loop

Town hall meetings are gatherings on the company's premises that all employees at a particular location are usually invited to. Their purpose is to allow top management to inform employees about actual change events, such as a merger or acquisition, or a new strategic direction. Although this dialogue format does not allow everybody to speak up, it provides an immediate experience of top management's current agenda and its implications for the business. An international pharmaceutical company established daily town hall meetings for a couple of months to accompany a major organisational change. Even though participation was voluntary, every morning almost 200 employees took advantage of this opportunity before going to their offices. The permanent access to top management and the latest developments created enormous trust in the leadership team amongst the workforce.

CEO breakfast – Forming an alliance

This format offers a personal casual meeting with the organisation's CEO to discuss a specific subject. It is less about information sharing; it is much more of a personal conversation about the subject and an exchange of perspectives. It is usually open for about 20 participants, creating an intimate atmosphere. The limitation of size means a selection process must be defined. A first-level criterion can be a certain organisational layer or a certain business unit. Within a defined target group, a next level of selection criterion needs to be established. Examples include: open application on a 'first come first serve' basis, or random selection by raffle.

Ambassador platforms – Supporting special agents

Organisations usually define specific roles within change management. This commonly includes the appointment of "change agents". Change agents are a group of managers who are taken out of everyday operations to commit a portion of their time to coordinating, facilitating and executing change-related activities. Special platforms for interaction and exchange, such as intranet-based portals, support change agents in their work. Ideally, change agents participate in a number of training sessions that introduce change-related tools and processes, and organisational change models, making them participate in dialogue formats and related train-the-trainer sessions. Change agents should be involved in planning and implementing cascading waves, and supporting managers in preparing for facilitating change-related activities.

Dialogue formats are often designed to allow feedback, be it input, questions or concerns. Change agents can play a vital part in gathering, analysing and channelling this feedback up to top-management, and in addressing reactions to change. In doing so, they ensure structured bottom-up communication.

Kick-off events – Enabling many-to-many conversations

Events require high investment. With this in mind, they need to offer participants more than a good time, great food and fancy gadgets. Events are an opportunity to bring people together, have them interact with top management, and let them mutually begin the change journey. Dialogue sessions amongst hundreds or thousands of employees and their top management become an unforgettable experience and offer a unique opportunity for information gathering and content creation.

The desired degree of involvement and exchange are influenced by the working mode and tools used.

- Roundtables with Learning Maps, for example, are an ideal tool for small teams. While the group members converse, the management can walk around and listen in.

- Tools like Open Space (where participants set topics themselves) and World Café (where people rotate between thematic tables) are suitable formats for more intense working modes, integrating all participants into the process of content creation.

- Kick-off events can be the starting point for cascading waves. Cascading toolkits with dialogue material similar to the ones just experienced during the event are an ideal support tool.

- Interactive media, such as digital voting systems and online chat rooms support the accumulation and consolidation of many small conversations and their outcomes – beyond the actual event.

Business simulations – Practice 'how to fly' before taking-off

Simulations are computer- or paper-based learning tools that depict the key characteristics of a business or industry: the business model, the key value drivers, typical interactions with customers, partners, suppliers and relevant Key Performance Indicators (KPIs) to measure business performance. Depending on their level of complexity, they can last between two hours to three days. They provide an ideal platform to model the complexities of an organisation's business environment. The helicopter view of business dynamics and the potential impact of strategic decisions on business performance help create a joint understanding of the 'big picture'. Playing out different scenarios enables participants to better understand the key drivers and dynamics of their changing business. This also helps to focus the dialogue on practicalities and potential obstacles during the change implementation. The competitive component, which is usually part of a simulation, creates an eagerness to win – and adds to the fun and excitement. This is one of the best prerequisites for encouraging engagement and learning.

Engagement throughout

Common to all these formats is that they ensure a high level of interaction between management and employees. Their purpose, scale, contents and duration, on the other hand, vary. Regardless of the format, a few fundamentals need to be met to ensure the effectiveness of the dialogue:

- The dialogue must convey a compelling story.
- The messages must be credible, consistent and relevant to the target audience.
- Management must play a key role in leading the dialogue.

Table 1 summarises the dialogue formats presented above with regard to their effectiveness along the entire change process.

Table 1. Dialogue formats and their effectiveness

	Creating a sense of urgency	Ensuring awareness & understanding	Empowering to act	Implementing change
Cascading waves	✓	✓	(✓)	✓
Town hall meetings	✓	✓	✗	✗
CEO breakfast	✓	✓	✗	✗
Ambassador Platforms	✓	✓	✓	✓
Kick-off events	✓	✓	✓	✗
Business simulations	✗	✗	✓	✓

Ideally, dialogue formats are deployed throughout each stage of the change process in order to demonstrate commitment and perseverance, and to sustain the momentum of engagement.

Impact of change communication

The evaluation of personal communication activities is widely known and applied (e.g. through evaluation sheets, manoeuvre critique). Assessing the impact of communication activities on business results is rarely done, even though this would seem to be a much better measure, since it illustrates the return on investment for change communications. An effective approach is to focus measurement on the key levers that support achieving the targeted results. If these key levers are identified, they become the cornerstone for a measurement dialogue.

Such measurement dialogues can be supported by "Diagnostic Tools". The format is that of a spidergram; its axes represent the defined key levers for success. For each key lever, a number of questions are developed that cover the most important aspects, such as critical behaviours, guidelines/procedures, capabilities, organisational structures and resources.

Prior to a critical communication intervention, the Diagnostic Tool is used to have a dialogue about the as-is situation. Within a team or unit, the questions for each lever are answered and rated on a qualitative scale which is linked to a numeric scoring. The average score is transferred onto the spidergram. Then, the to-be assessment is discussed. It defines the areas for improvement and provides the basis for defining action steps during the implementation of the change.

The as-is and to-be assessments should be repeated within the next three to six months, or whenever appropriate. Alternatively, the monitoring of the spidergram may become a regular agenda point during team meetings. In this way, the Diagnostic Tool itself becomes a dialogue platform that steers a relevant debate about what should be achieved and how.

Start talking

Whether dialogue is part of change communication or not provides an indication of the culture in which change is supposed to happen. Arguments like "We can't bother management with that" say something about management's intentions and commitment. Why, then, bother employees? Openness, credibility and commitment support change – and so does dialogue. Dialogue formats as a change communication tool provide numerous benefits. And each organisation needs to create a suitable mix of activities and formats for every change process. However, it is not the number of dialogues that matters. It is management's commitment to host dialogues that makes the difference. A task that is not up for delegation!

Use of multipliers in change communication: How credible personal communication can make change effective

Eike Wagner

During organisational change, face-to-face communication with the employees who are affected is a key factor for success. Typical interventions in change processes include kick-off events, management meetings and workshops. Given the limitations of these interventions, the preparation of credible communicators from different hierarchical levels and organisational units, as multipliers, is an effective alternative. Based on extensive research and practical experience in multinational companies such as BMW and Siemens, this article explains, using seven questions, how to choose and prepare those multipliers and how to integrate them into different communication activities.

The use of multipliers is not just another communications activity, but an approach to communication. It is a way of increasing the overall effectiveness of a communications programme, if other means of face-to-face communication with employees on lower levels are limited in one way or another. Opportunities for personal communication between top management and employees are limited by availability constraints on top management. Personal communication between middle management and employees can be problematic when middle managers do not sufficiently support the change, which is frequently the case. Although direct supervisors are usually the preferred source of information for employees, their level of understanding of the change is often not sufficient to encourage them to accept the change.

The use of multipliers addresses these limitations in two ways. First, the credibility and accuracy of the information cascaded up and down the hierarchy is increased by giving multipliers a formal role in these communication activities. Second, those responsible for the change are provided with an alternative to personal communication via the management cascade. A separate network of communicators from different levels and units is created for the purpose of the change project.

A multiplier approach is particularly appropriate when a change affects several elements of an organisation (e.g. strategy, structure, systems and/or processes), and when a change requires communication to a large number of employees at different locations over a long period of time. This is because face-to-face communication is more important when the change is a major one, and the return on the time and money invested in the preparation of multipliers is higher when multipliers are used in several communication activities over a certain period of time.

What is the multiplier approach and what is it not?

The essence of the multiplier approach is to prepare employees from different units and levels to play a central role in communication relating to a specific change. Multipliers are chosen and prepared for the purpose of spreading an accurate understanding and favourable attitude towards the change. Related terms are ambassadors, apostles, best-practice scouts or blockbusters. The difference between the specific concept of multiplier and the more general concept of opinion leader is that opinion leaders are expected to influence others' opinions by the nature of their formal or informal relationships. The challenge in change projects is that opinion leaders always lead opinions – either in favour or disfavour of the change.

Where does it apply in practice?

A multinational automotive company wanted to implement a new recruiting process and technology across all its locations in Germany. 70,000 employees – spread across five big and several small locations – were affected by the change in different ways. The challenge for the project team was to ensure that all people affected by the change would behave as assumed in the business case on the project. The project team knew that the investment of €10 million would not lead to the desired cost reduction of €13 million if employees did not adapt to the new process quickly and use the new technology adequately.

The idea behind the multiplier approach was to explain the change to one group after another, to make them accept the change, and to show them how to act in the future. The 50 multipliers were the key in bridging the gap between the ten people in the project team and the 1,000 people in the next group. A clearly defined communication cascade in addition to the existing communication structure was created temporarily for the implementation of this one project.

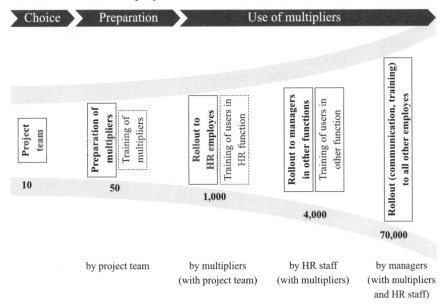

Fig. 1. Multiplier approach applied to the introduction of new HR process

What is the role of multipliers?

Multipliers should be credible communicators and thereby increase the effectiveness of communication activities. Their overall responsibility is to contribute to creating understanding and acceptance among those affected by the change.

In order to ensure that the multiplier approach has the desired effect, multipliers should have the following specific responsibilities.

1. They should help those responsible for implementation with the fine-tuning of the central implementation plan.
2. They should develop the local implementation plan. This will integrate the views of peripheral locations into the planning process.
3. They should play an active role in communicating the change. They should explain the change and answer the other employees' questions.

4. They should facilitate the top-down and bottom-up communication between those responsible for the change and those affected by the change. They should diplomatically mediate between the views of the project team and the users of the new process and technology.
5. They should have a 'translation function' in that they tailor information to the specific situation in their unit. They can answer the questions that employees tend to ask in change processes such as: "What does the introduction of the new process mean for us at our location?"

How much time do multipliers need?

The amount of time multipliers need to fulfil their role depends on the complexity of the change and the ratio between multipliers and other employees affected by the change. As a rule of thumb, the workload of multipliers should not exceed three days per week, because otherwise multipliers would not be able to do their regular jobs. Of course, multipliers' regular tasks have to be reduced anyway, but removing multipliers from their normal responsibilities would cause several problems.

1. They would no longer be affected by the change themselves, thus making it more difficult to understand the impact of the change.
2. They would be less credible as communicators because they would be seen as part of the implementation team and not one of those affected.
3. It would be more difficult to reintegrate them into the new structure after the change has been implemented.

The actual workload of multipliers is likely to vary during the implementation process – with likely peaks in the preparation phase and during the central communication waves.

How to choose multipliers?

The effectiveness of the multiplier approach depends on who is chosen as a multiplier. In order to fulfil their role as credible communicators, multipliers need to be accepted by the other employees and have a certain level of communication skills.

The following specific characteristics are particularly relevant.

1. Multipliers need to be personally affected by the change.
2. They need to be part of the employee group that they are expected to address – for example, the same function, location or level.

3. They need to have the intellectual capability to understand the change and its impact within a reasonable timeframe.

These characteristics increase the likelihood that multipliers will be willing and able to explain the change and that the other employees will perceive multipliers as "one of us". This so-called in-group bias – together with a history of personal interaction between multipliers and the other employees – are two key factors influencing the perceived credibility of a communicator. Furthermore, being affected by the change yourself and being part of the same group as the other employees is a prerequisite for understanding the other employees' concerns and uncertainties. Finally, employees from the same group speak the same language as their colleagues and have similar background knowledge.

4. Multipliers need to have the communication skills needed to explain the change.
5. They need to have the ability to network, in order to reach a sufficient number of people personally.

These characteristics will ensure that multipliers have a level of communication skills that can be built on in the preparation phase. Without these basic skills, the time available for preparation will not be sufficient.

Choosing employees from different locations as multipliers is necessary because other employees do not know the location well enough, and they are not sufficiently available to answer questions. Furthermore, we suggest a mixture of functions. In the above-mentioned project, 80 percent of the multipliers were recruiters from central or local recruiting departments, and 20 percent came from other functions in HR. This was beneficial because "recruiters are the experts [... whereas] other HR employees usually have better connections to the managers in the other departments" as the responsible change manager concluded.

With regard to the process of choosing multipliers, different approaches are available. First, the head of a unit can ask specific employees on the basis of the desired characteristics of multipliers, whether they would like to become a multiplier. Second, it is often appropriate to choose the employees who would be affected first by the new system or process. Although this choice can be very practical, implementers have to make sure that these employees have the required communication skills. Third, employees themselves can choose the multiplier because this increases the likelihood that the other employees in the unit will accept the multiplier. This approach needs to be used with caution insofar as employees tend to choose the multiplier on grounds other than those required for a successful multiplier approach. The appropriateness of the different approaches will depend on the specific situation of the project. In the above-mentioned project, all three approaches were used because the responsible line managers at different locations had different views on the issue, and those responsible for implementation wanted to take these views into account. This is important because, in any project, choosing a multiplier requires negotiation with the potential multiplier's line manager. Can you image any line manager allowing an employee to become a multiplier without seeing the benefit of the multiplier approach for his/her unit or without having a clear idea about the amount of time required for the role?

How to prepare multipliers?

Imagine the following situation: an employee asks a multiplier, "What do you think about the change?" and the multiplier says, "It's good but I haven't really understood it." This would be funny if it was not an actual statement by a respondent in an evaluation of a multiplier approach in a recent case of restructuring. A multiplier must know a lot more than the other employees. The preparation of multipliers in terms of their understanding and acceptance of the change – as well as their willingness and capability to be a multiplier – is therefore the key to success. Although there are different ways of preparing multipliers, several key points became evident in all our experience in different projects. Fig. 2 illustrates how preparation influences the behaviour adopted by multipliers during the implementation process and thus the overall success of the change project.

The responsibility of multipliers should be discussed during the selection procedure. It should be included in the invitation to the first multiplier workshop, repeated at the beginning of the workshop, and there should be enough time for discussion and questions throughout the workshop. It is important that multipliers have clear answers to questions such as "What exactly am I supposed to do?", "How does the process continue?" or "Who must contact whom to make arrangements?"

Clarifying the roles is not only important when it comes to the effectiveness of the multiplier approach but also with regard to its efficiency. In one of our projects, multipliers did not know that certain tools would be provided by the project team, so they first collected ideas for a presentation and designing an event. This duplication of work could have been avoided. Multipliers had even made appointments with colleagues to discuss this further and it took a lot of effort to clear up this misunderstanding with the respective colleagues.

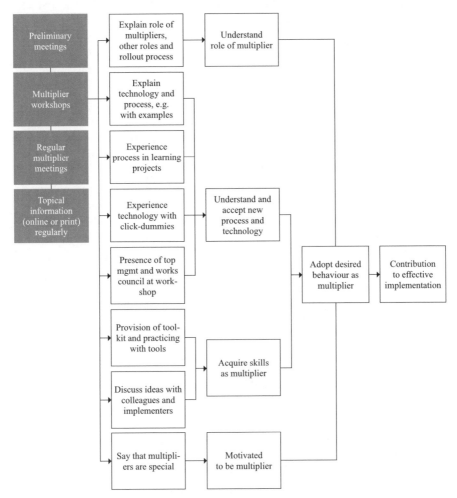

Fig. 2. Different ways of preparing multipliers and their likely effects

At least one face-to-face workshop with all multipliers is a must, with two workshops probably being the best trade-off between costs and desired effect. In the above-mentioned project, we designed two workshops with two months in-between. The first workshop focused on clarifying the role of multipliers and creating an understanding of the change. The second workshop built on the first and focused on developing the capabilities for carrying the change into the HR departments.

It is obvious that multipliers need to understand and accept the new process and technology, because they have to promote it to their colleagues in the different departments. One way to achieve this is to explain the new process using presentations and illustrations. Another is to use experiential learning projects, so that multipliers can experience what it would be like to work within the new structure – to be an employee in recruiting, an HR manager, a manager from another department, or an applicant. When a new technology is involved, a draft version of the new technology can be another way to enable multipliers to understand and accept the new process and technology. These so-called click-dummies have limited functionality, but multipliers see the screens and learn about the most important functions. The click-dummies should be presented in a group session, and afterwards computers should be available so that multipliers can practise on their own whenever they want to.

Another factor that influences multipliers' perception of the change is their view on who supports the change. Therefore, the presence of a member of the top management team and the project leader shows that the change is important and that multipliers play an important role in the implementation of the change. Furthermore, multipliers may also want to know whether the heads of the various regional offices or the works council support the change. In the above-mentioned project, a multiplier rightly asked, "How can this work if the works council and the head of the HR department don't support it?"

The provision of a toolkit (Fig. 3) is a must to enable multipliers to learn the skills required for a successful multiplier approach. A toolkit is intended to support multipliers by providing the required background information and specific guidance for completing their tasks. A standard presentation provides an overview of the change – including the terminology to use. Appropriate answers to FAQs add to the presentation insofar as multipliers are able to present the change (one-way communication) and also answer the other employees' questions (two-way communication). Suggestions for workshop designs ensure the consistency of implementation activities across locations and save time in the planning phase. The specific tools will depend on the requirements of the respective change project. A general piece of advice is: do not be afraid of making the toolkit very detailed, because different multipliers need different kinds of support.

In addition to being provided with tools, multipliers need to practice using the tools. Multipliers are not specifically chosen for their communication skills and therefore may find it difficult to give a presentation without detailed preparation. Typical feedback we receive at the end of workshops is: "It was very important for me that I was able to give the presentation during the workshop and that I received feedback from the other multipliers." Applying the different tools not only increases familiarity with the tools but also increases understanding of the new process: after all, multipliers really have to understand the new process before they can present it to their colleagues at the workshop.

#	Content	Page
1	Information about the toolkit	3
2	Rollout masterplan	6
3	My role as a multiplier	7
4	Training measures	8
5	Workshops in HR departments	9
6	Presentation for HR departments	30
7	Presentation for other departments	41
8	Guideline on how to use click-dummies	52
9	Likely questions and appropriate answers	54
10	Comparison of old and new recruiting process	63
11	List of contacts	108

Fig. 3. Table of contents of toolkit in sample project

After initial preparation, multipliers need ongoing support throughout the change process. This is best achieved through a combination of regular face-to-face meetings and topical information about the development of the project. Regular information updates (for example, sent every two weeks by email or letter) keep multipliers informed about the change. It is useful to leave space at the end of the toolkit to insert these updates. The aims of regular multiplier meetings may vary during the project. At the beginning, multipliers may need additional guidance and to share experiences with their colleagues. Later in the process, specific interventions such as a series of road shows or a training workshop can be planned in detail to ensure consistency across locations. Even further on in the process, first reviews can be conducted and multipliers may need to be motivated to stay focused.

How to integrate multipliers into communication activities?

The influence of the multiplier approach on the effectiveness of the communication programme depends on the integration of multipliers into existing communication activities and on the design of additional change interventions around the multiplier approach.

Multipliers can explain specific aspects of the change at the kick-off event at their location and thereby enhance the credibility of the information. For example, they can convince the other employees that the new form of cooperation between headquarters and local departments also has a positive side, or that the new technology is better than the rumours say. In the above-mentioned project, the kick-off event was followed by a series of local events at most locations. During these events, multipliers supported the project team in their explanation of the details of the change by tailoring the information to the situation at their location. Multipliers were able to use their own experience during the multiplier workshops, saying that initial scepticism is normal but that the new process certainly has positive aspects. Furthermore, multipliers were integrated into workshops with representatives from different departments; these were organised by the project team to discuss the impact of the change on the structure in different locations.

Depending on the ratio between multipliers and other employees affected by the change, multipliers can also directly pass on information to the colleagues in their departments if enough time for presentations is reserved during the regular team meetings. Team meetings without the participation of multipliers are unlikely to be effective, because group leaders are often insufficiently informed about the change to explain it to their employees and to answer employees' questions. Ideally, multipliers attend the regular meetings of different teams on a rotating basis throughout the change process. This creates the variety of possibilities for dialogue which is important in the context of organisational change.

Multipliers can also have a beneficial effect in print and online communication. The credibility of the information provided can be increased using statements, quotes and pictures of multipliers on a poster, newsletter or website. However, the success of this approach again depends on how well multipliers are prepared. In one of our projects, implementers expected multipliers to distribute the newsletters to their colleagues, but the multipliers did not behave as intended due to a lack of preparation. As a result, the newsletter did not reach all the employees, and they were not encouraged to read the newsletter.

Finally, the use of multipliers can compensate for a lack of formal communication. In one of our projects, multipliers at different locations had to explain the need for change in endless informal discussions, because the project team had failed to create an awareness of the change during the kick-off event. Furthermore, multipliers can be the central contact for questions about the change at each location, they can actively forward topical information or refer to additional information material.

How to measure the success of the multiplier approach?

The benefit of the multiplier approach is as difficult to measure as the effect of most communication activities. The results are hardly apparent, but are rather 'in the heads' of those affected by the change. In our projects, statements made by responsible line managers and employees affected by the change clearly indicate the benefit of the multiplier approach. I personally conducted two case studies over a period of two and a half years – including observations of workshops in which multipliers participated and over 100 interviews with employees affected by the change. Typical statements on the role of multipliers in communication activities were: "This was the first time that I understood what they want from us" and "She really represents our opinion at project meetings".

In organisational practice, there are two ways to monitor the effect of the multiplier approach. First, questions on multipliers can be integrated into evaluations of the communication activities in which they participate. For example, a questionnaire that is distributed after an event can include questions on the different speakers. The same approach can be used for workshops or seminars. Second, a change monitor that is regularly updated should include questions on how well employees understand and accept the change. If there has been an increase in understanding, this is likely to be a result of the communication activities that have taken place since the last change-monitor update – the multipliers' influence can then be deduced. If necessary, an audit of the different communication activities can be conducted, for example to justify the costs triggered by the use of multipliers. A mix of questionnaires and semi-structured interviews provides both quantitative and qualitative data on the benefit of multipliers.

Benefits

The use of a multiplier approach can significantly increase the effectiveness of change communication and thereby facilitate the successful implementation of top-down change. Specific benefits of a multiplier approach include:

- an additional channel of personal communication
- compensation for the limitations of communication via line management
- high level awareness of the change through regular communication
- authenticity and credibility of the information
- information tailored to the requirements of the different target groups

- positive influence on the accuracy of informal communication
- money savings generated by higher motivation and less resistance

Lessons learned

- Take the time to choose the right multipliers (capability + willingness).
- Prepare multipliers adequately (role + know-how + tools + skills).
- Use teams of two multipliers for the first communication activities so that they can support each other and become more confident.
- Schedule the last preparation workshop after the first activities in order to learn from these experiences and to adjust if necessary.
- Install small learning groups to ensure ongoing exchange and mutual (technical and emotional) learning between multipliers.
- Make sure that a member of the top management team attends multiplier meetings from time to time to keep the level of motivation and commitment high and to learn from the view of multipliers.
- After the first wave of communication activities, clarify the role of multipliers during the later stages of the implementation process.
- Do not use a multiplier approach if you are not willing to invest the necessary time and money into the preparation of multipliers.

Why engagement matters – From command and control to collective learning via social software

Sabine Stecher

The ability to change in ever-shorter time periods has become a key factor for economic success. This applies equally to multinational organisations and to their staff. In this context, the limits of a command-and-control approach by management, or a tell-and-sell approach in corporate communication, soon become clear in a change process, so that such methods rarely achieve the desired success. Employee engagement and communication approaches that do justice to the needs and desires of managers and staff make sustainable successful change processes possible. Social software can be an essential tool of engagement contributing to the success of change processes.

"You just can't impose command-and-control mechanisms on a large, highly professional workforce. [...] The CEO can't say to them, 'Get in line and follow me.' Or 'I've decided what your values are.' They're too smart for that. And as you know, smarter people tend to be, well, a little more challenging; you might even say cynical" (Palmisano 2004). What Samuel J. Palmisano, Chairman of the Board and CEO at IBM, has to say here about management in general is all the more valid for change and transformation processes. When company executives and external advisors develop strategies, processes and decisions behind closed doors, the staff quickly feel insufficiently informed and robbed of any opportunity to get involved. Important staff members often resign as a result. "Technology, speed and access have created a sophisticated and cynical knowledge worker who demands honesty and two-way, adult-to-adult dialogue in return for buy-in to the business direction" (Moorcroft 2006). The way companies communicate with managers and staff makes a decisive contribution to the success or failure of the change project. "Without the kind of communication that supports participation, the script for change, which is crucial for giving the people involved a sense of direction, will remain abstract and empty. Likewise, successful change will not become firmly and permanently established without the joint consolidation of, reflection on, and passing on, of new processes and behaviour patterns, which can also only be generated by communication" (Langen 2007).

Engagement in change processes

Engagement – Ideology or a measurable strategy for success?

It is undisputed that the command-and-control approach has had its day in global, highly flexible and sophisticated working environments. The psychological contract between employers and employees – a secure job in return for compliance and loyalty – is becoming less and less popular on both sides. Back in 2004, the change specialist John Smythe was commissioned by McKinsey to examine how companies try to involve their staff in change processes in a study called "Engaging people at work to drive strategy and change" (Smythe 2004a). Smythe revealed four different corporate approaches – each of which had a different effect on staff behaviour:

1. Telling the many what has been decided by the few – outcome: hooligans or spectators
2. Selling to the many what has been decided by the few – outcome: compliant collaborators
3. Driving accountability down by implicating people as individuals – outcome: willing collaborators
4. Co-creation: working with those who will add value if included in decision forming and change/strategy development – outcome: personally committed reformers.

According to Smythe, engagement approaches aimed at co-creation are sustainably successful: "Employee engagement means opening up decision making and change to those who will add value, not faster, more persuasive propaganda. [...] Employee engagement is significantly driven by the degree to which people are usefully included in the decision-making process both day-to-day and in big-ticket change, crisis and transformation" (Smythe 2007). The aim is to make optimum use of the staff's potential: the staff are encouraged to think about value-adding measures and to exercise constructive criticism. As a result, they are more creative, more productive and "make other people's change their own" (Smythe 2007). They often already know from their daily work which key adjustments need to be made for optimisation, strategic reorientation or the specific challenges of corporate integration. Engagement also facilitates the networking of knowledge in the company: companies that provide platforms for the exchange of ideas and information between management and staff, as well as among the staff themselves, are automatically promoting knowledge transfer. Staff feel they are appreciated, and this has a positive effect on their motivation, their behaviour towards customers and their loyalty in complex change processes. "It is not a question of all involvement being good; rather it is a question of whether value will be added if up front involvement makes for a better solution" (Smythe 2004b). We can thus conclude that engagement makes sense from a business point of view – it pays off. When considering a decision for or against involving staff in change processes, therefore, the ideological and functional levels should be kept strictly separate (Trebesch 2007).

Fig. 1. Differences in justifying the involvement of the people affected (Trebesch 2007)

Level of engagement

Smythe's conclusion is that engagement is primarily a matter of management philosophy: it determines the kind of management that is "based on the idea of including the right people in the right decisions at the right time in the right way" (Smythe 2007). In complex change processes, it is precisely this approach that can decide whether implementation is successful or not. When familiar structures are abolished and planning is uncertain, fear and resistance often develop at the level of middle management and below. If corporate processes are to be made more dynamic, decision-making processes on all levels have to be accelerated. New strategies and methods must be applied and new work relations and workflows tested by the staff in experimental environments; instruments for monitoring success and quality have to be reviewed or new ones found. Teams that are used to working together often disband to form more flexible task forces or expert networks.

How high the degree of employee engagement should be in this situation depends, on the one hand, on the kind of staff structure and management culture that prevails, how the actual corporate culture is practised, and to what extent staff are already involved in decision-making. On the other hand, the specific challenges of the change process must be taken into consideration: the involvement of the staff will not be as intense in a restructuring process that must be concluded within a short time as in a transformation process aimed at reorienting corporate strategy.[1]

An engagement approach that is consistently geared to the aims of change management integrates several forms of management control. The overall process remains controlled in a top-down fashion, while incorporating bottom-up and/or side-to-side elements. It can be a good idea to select different approaches for different target groups. Individual people – e.g. defined change agents – play a key role in creating a trusting environment and provide impulses for the change.[2]

---

[1] The contribution by Joachim Klewes and Ralf Langen in this volume describes how to differentiate between different types of change and how to illustrate them.

[2] See the contributions in this volume by Robert Wreschniok, "The power of ideas – Reputation management and successful change" and Eike Wagner, "Use of multipliers in change communication".

Engagement and communication

A communication strategy that does justice to the challenges of change processes and relies on engagement will be moving in an area of tension between control and commitment: in order to reduce complexity and maintain an overview, the management level often develops a need for clearly regulated and controllable communication approaches, such as telling and selling. At the same time, the limits of this approach can soon become clear if new working relations are constantly forming. Clear-cut responsibilities and attitudes often have only temporary validity during restructuring; different levels of knowledge and contrary opinions on strategies or priorities collide.

In change processes, members of staff must be able to familiarise themselves with new tasks and areas of knowledge independently and increasingly take on mediating communication tasks, thus taking some of the pressure off management. They have to keep a confusing and changing number of people informed, be able to judge which new or abolished project groups or corporate divisions are affected by their work, and constantly adjust targets, strategies and communication rules to the change process. In addition to operational business, a lot of additional work crops up which – over the entire course of a change process – can only be borne by staff with a lot of commitment. Numerous socio-psychological studies document how this necessary commitment can be strengthened. They show that change processes are only successful if the staff are ready to get involved. Typical forms of resistance against innovations can only be broken down if the staff feel that they are personally involved in the process, that their fears and questions are taken seriously, and if they can contribute ideas and suggestions of their own.[3] When staff are given a chance to take part in the change process by taking on sophisticated tasks, they feel part of the company, personally responsible for the success of the project; their performance is recognised. The growing demands on staff's self-management are likely to further increase this need.

Marketing-like internal communication approaches are increasingly regarded as being 'out'. This is also confirmed in a study by Insidedge-GolinHarris, published in 2006, on what staff expect from internal communications. According to this, key ways to make employees "more satisfied, productive and committed" are to:

---

[3] See the contribution by Marit Gerkhardt, Dieter Frey and Peter Fischer in this volume: "The human factor in change processes".

- "Create a free and open environment where all feel comfortable expressing opinions, ideas and suggestions
- Be more open, honest and straight-forward, even when communicating
  difficult or bad news
- Share information and communicate in a timely manner [...]
- Communicate more frequently, regularly and in different ways" (Insidedge-GolinHarris 2006b).

In the increasingly complex working environment, and especially in
change processes, this can only be partially achieved with traditional
measures. Smythe goes further: what is needed is "a complete rewrite of
the way organisations communicate and engage with leaders and employees" (Smythe 2007).

A movement is already becoming established in communication technology that takes the need for involvement into account and suggests possible solutions for the communication tasks of the engagement approach:
the development of social software. Many members of staff already use
these interactive media privately; the staff of tomorrow will probably regard them as standard. Companies must therefore ask themselves to what
extent they can – or would like to – already use these technologies mean-
ingfully today in their communication strategy. Up to now, companies
have shown "widespread but careful interest in this trend", according to
the 2007 McKinsey global survey on "How businesses are using Web 2.0".
"Expressing satisfaction with their Internet investments so far, they say
that Web 2.0 technologies are strategic and that they plan to increase these
investments. But companies aren't necessarily relying on the best-known
Web 2.0 trends, such as blogs; instead, they place the greatest importance
on technologies that enable automation and networking" (McKinsey
2007).[4]

Social software as an engagement tool in change processes

Social software as a work platform

Blogs, wikis and other applications from the world of Web 2.0 seem tailor-
made for engagement approaches in change processes: "All social software

---

[4] The surveyed companies use Web 2.0 tools to communicate with customers and
business partners and to strengthen internal cooperation.

is founded on a non-IT social system that human beings use anyway. [...] Social media merely allows the interaction to happen over a technology platform instead" (Bryant 2007). The users individually compile contents and tools in user-friendly structures and are permanently further developing the applications. People, not IT, are the focus.[5]

As a direct communication technology requiring little maintenance or updating, social software enables quick coordination between staff, the easy briefing of a changing number of participants, continuous insight into the current status of discussions, and speedy documentation of the work processes. Information needed to continue working productively can be retrieved at all times. Social software offers a platform for informal exchanges on results and experience with new strategies and working methods; it makes it possible to find experts in the staff pool and to jointly look for solutions to current problems or failures. Social software thus also contributes towards optimising knowledge transfer and further training.

Paradigm shift in corporate communication

Social software can encourage a paradigm shift in corporate communication – from 'top-down' to 'side-to-side':

- The staff are equal communication partners: the communication department provides platforms and tools; the staff supply the content and share their information themselves.
- The process of editing content is replaced by guidelines for use.
- The frequency of exchanges is governed not by defined communication plans, but by the staff in their use of the system.
- The results are evaluated not by the communication department, but by the staff themselves: they decide what they use (and how) and what they don't use.

Social software thus relieves management and project management of mediating communication tasks and enables staff to better and more quickly delegate tasks themselves. However, this will only succeed if the company decides to adopt co-creation and to accept different, sometimes critical views. This does not mean doing without control mechanisms completely and leaving everything to uncontrolled communication. The basic rules of vocational interaction – such as professionalism or respect – remain in

---

[5] Tim O'Reilly (2005) formulated the basic principle of this development: "Web 2.0 doesn't have a hard boundary, but rather a gravitational core. You can visualize Web 2.0 as a set of principles and practices [...]."

force in informal communication formats. Companies such as IBM, GM and the World Bank[6] rely on guidelines and codes of conduct in this context. One effective basic rule, for example, is to ban anonymous contributions. This means that every member of staff is responsible for his/her contribution and therefore has an interest in maintaining the quality standard. People who violate the rules of behaviour can be punished by having their access blocked. The business focus can remain very pronounced if, for example, the company asks for feedback specifically from field service, only allows discussion on selected business issues, or strictly separates project communication from the informal exchanges on topical questions and problems.

The difference between this and classic corporate communication lies in the kind of application used. Ross Chestney, Head of Communications Services at British Telecom, puts it in a nutshell: "These tools are not about push. They're not about driving. The very point of them is bottom-up control. As a communicator, you provide, you shape, you set guidance and you enable. That's it. The audience then decides what's useful and what's not" (Melcrum 2007). Another difference lies in the way the tools are introduced. Not all staff are familiar with new Web 2.0 technologies. It has therefore proven beneficial to continue using and extending existing structures, e.g. by publishing staff articles in existing online publications or creating a section for employee collaboration and interaction in the familiar intranet. Key people for the implementation of social software should be staff who benefit directly from the new technology. They are given the new software as an experimental solution, are trained in the use of the application, invited to experiment themselves, suggest extensions and get involved in decisions on implementation and uses. Furthermore, the staff must be given support in learning to use the new software and time to apply it. Evaluation processes should take into account that a certain amount of time is needed before a critical mass of participants and contributions is reached.

2.0 = Too much effort and 0 results?

Internal communicators see the greatest benefit of social software in "improved employee engagement" (71%), "improved internal collaboration"

---

[6] Melcrum (2007) conducted a survey into social media adoption by large corporations worldwide. More than 2,100 executives responded about how blogs, podcasts, wikis and other collaborative technologies are being used to communicate with employees and customers.

(59%), the "development of internal communities" (51%) and creating "a two-way dialogue with senior executives" (47%) (Melcrum 2007). Because it has not been in use for very long, reliable figures are not yet available on the extent to which the use of social software contributes financially or strategically to a company's value added.

Companies that have already introduced social software use different 2.0 tools, depending on their corporate culture. Here are some examples:

- To begin with, the brewery group Scottish & Newcastle set up a regular Big Debate on its intranet with broad-ranging and challenging questions. "Readers can click beside the question and register their views and opinions. The responses are moderated before being posted on a separate page of the site – a form of 'have your say' across the company" (Melcrum 2007).
- IBM uses collaborative wikis, blogs for certain target groups and special themes (e.g. executive blogging, relationship blogging, issue blogging, product blogging) with internal blogging guidelines, jams, RSS, podcasts, videocasting and virtual-world technologies like Second Life (Melcrum 2007).
- American Electric Power (AEP) set up a section for employee collaboration on its intranet: "It includes a weekly multiple-choice poll, enabling employees to quickly register their opinions on company or societal issues; a weekly discussion with a carefully chosen topic of broad appeal, soliciting employee perspectives and ideas, in full text; an online thank-you card application" for colleagues, and a popular online marketplace which "gets employees into the habit of sharing and exchanging" (Melcrum 2007).
- "Microsoft [UK] has employed a number of social media tools within the organisation and is using them successfully to help cut down on information overload" (Melcrum 2007).

Dialogue-based communication with a heterogeneous pool of recipients can have a standardising effect on all internal communication. For example, it makes it necessary to agree on certain terms and definitions and understandable ways of formulating ideas. By using threads, tags and full-text searches, social software generates a level of clarity that is resistant to organisational and strategic restructuring measures in the company. Information remains easy to find.

Social software in change communication

Social software can be used in various areas in change processes. In mergers and acquisitions, the tools support the work of the project management office, for example by promptly informing project participants in many different areas and locations about the current status of the project and by providing rapid consultation processes. The staff are also regularly informed about the course of the process and its results and can easily make contact with their new colleagues. In transformation processes, it extends the possible areas of involvement and to some extent itself becomes a driver of change. Like at IBM, for example: "It reflects the very way IBM does business, rather than the type of business it does: increasingly less command-and-control, top-driven and hierarchical, it's spent the last decade developing towards a consultancy model of business – with individuals moving fluidly across the organisation and its structures. 'It means that a more democratic concept of communication – with content driven and contributed from any level of the organisation – is the right medium for us'" (Melcrum 2007).

Social software can be used for the key communication tasks of creating attention, informing, involving and collaborating in the change process:

Creating attention: To mark the kick-off of a change project (e.g. day one of a new company, the launch of the culture process), when the staff boot up their computers in the morning they are first greeted by the CEO in a podcast. She or he explains 'face-to-face' the need for the change process, appeals for the cooperation of every individual, and in this way creates what John P. Kotter calls the necessary 'sense of urgency' (Kotter 1996). Further podcasts follow at certain milestones during the project with current assessments and initial success reports. Various spokespersons should be given a chance to speak – above all, the defined change agents from the management coalition for the change. In this way – via the personal commitment of important opinion leaders – it becomes clear that the change really is taking place in all areas and is supported by the key people. After several acquisitions, Scottish & Newcastle used a video newsletter made 'by the people for the people' to promote a 'one team' culture: members of staff presented several features on a CD, which was then distributed to all locations worldwide (Melcrum 2007).

Informing: Not being sufficiently informed remains one of the most frequent criticisms by staff in the context of change processes. Social software can be used in many different ways for managing knowledge. McAfee examined suitable functions of social software for corporate knowledge management, calling them 'SLATES' (McAfee 2006). They are also valid for change projects:

- Search: staff tend to use keywords more than navigation structures and help windows when searching (McAfee 2006). Accordingly, the search function should also show the contents of the informal intranet pages such as blogs and wikis.
- Links: "Links are an excellent guide to what's important and provide structure to online content. In this structure, the 'best' pages are the ones that are most frequently linked to" (McAfee 2006). To make this organisational principle possible in the company, a lot of people must have a chance to add links. In this way, the staff themselves can connect the contents of the current change project with the established information.
- Authoring: "Internet blogs and Wikipedia have shown that many people have a desire to author – to write for a broad audience. [... M]ost people have something to contribute, whether it's knowledge, insight, experience, a comment, a fact, an edit, a link, and so on, and authorship is a way to elicit these contributions" (McAfee 2006). Especially in the case of optimisation programs (e.g. customer orientation, supply chain), companies should use their staff's experience as a (or: their most) valuable source.
- Tags: many staff would like intranet content to be better categorised. Tags enable staff to set keywords, thus reflecting their use habits and revealing which sites are visited most frequently, i.e. are most relevant for the internal target groups of change communication.
- Extensions: categorisation can be partially automated by algorithms – the computer recommends the user further offers 'by extension' based on her or his usage habits. For example, it could suggest participation in a value jam to a member of staff reading the Corporate Values.
- Signals: to avoid missing interesting updates, signals – in the form of email alerts or RSS-Feeds – inform the staff member when new information is added to predefined sites. This ensures that heterogeneous target groups are provided with information simultaneously – even in highly dynamic change processes.

Involving and collaborating: Blogs and wikis, for example, facilitate speedy and regular exchanges of information and more between the project teams and all affected members of staff. They reduce email traffic, which often gets out of control in change processes; they also integrate groups of staff into the community who are more remote, for example, work at distant locations. User behaviour shows that wikis and blogs are signs not of a collective mass movement, but of division of labour and specialisation

(Mayer-Schönberger 2007). Jams – i.e. real-time, online idea-sharing sessions – are especially useful in culture processes: the broad discussion quickly reveal what impressions staff members really have of their company's corporate identity and whether the company's (new) values and objectives are important for them. This may seem risky, but it is the first, necessary step towards really establishing the desired new corporate culture. As early as 2001, IBM conducted a multimedia brainstorming session under the title World Jam in the context of a reorientation of corporate strategy: 50,000 members of staff took part worldwide; similar jams followed (Melcrum 2007).

Chances and risks of social software in change communication

Social software in corporate communication means a shift in the control opportunities available to communicators and management. Staff are increasingly incorporated into communication and decision-making processes, get together independently to form teams via social software tools, share their know-how, delegate tasks, discuss management decisions and formulate targets and opinions. In order to avoid a weakening of corporate values that are already established, discussion areas should be clearly limited to areas of change. Often the introduction of social software is only a reaction of the company to what is already happening among staff – e.g. blogs. If the company also offers and structures blogs and optimises their application, this makes a certain degree of regulation possible. At the same time, staff members make their know-how, specific interests and engagement for corporate culture transparent through the public discussion. The assessment and selection of staff for certain tasks – e.g. as change agents – can then be based on a more solid foundation. Monitoring ongoing work processes makes it possible to intervene at an early stage when problems, delays or conflicts arise. This makes it possible to already carry out an evaluation – for example, of the staff's commitment – during the change process.

The risks of social software in change processes are the same as in all internal measures that reduce top management's control over their staff. Working on the 'internal is external' principle, communicators must prepare for situations in which critical information will reach the general public, where they will be picked up to serve all kinds of vested interests. The media can make money with information that criticises the company; competitors will try to directly exploit leaks about problems to their own advantage – especially in change situations. And the capital market will punish any sudden loss of confidence thus caused with share-price mark-downs. Every company's management has to decide for itself whether it believes that these risks offset the sustainable positive effects of a participatory culture and, specifically, the use of corresponding instruments.

Cultural bridges

International mergers, joint ventures, acquisitions, outsourcing or the development of new locations all require intercultural interaction – not only between national cultures, but also between the cultures of organisations. The differences between the corporate cultures are more likely to be based on people's practices than their values (Hofstede 2001). Social software facilitates interaction and can help global teams to work together and to communicate better with each other. "At IBM, for example, every tool introduced is there to support the way global employees connect with each other" (Melcrum 2007). "Once following a classic multinational model of business, IBM has been refocusing the business over the last 10 years to something more along the lines of the 'global integrated enterprise' – a networked organisation, with the walls between business lines torn down and a fluid employee base who can operate across functions, sectors and geographies. 'That means that social media must absolutely reflect where the company is going'" (Melcrum 2007).

Conclusion

The engagement approach and the introduction of social software do not mean a free-for-all democracy. The aim is not to allow the staff to participate in everything, but to use their creativity and involvement to increase corporate value. This benefits both sides: the staff feel both challenged and encouraged by sophisticated tasks; management control of complex change projects comes closer to the reality of corporate processes and is given greater backing. As a fundamental management philosophy, a switch towards staff engagement in itself means major changes for all levels of the company: the management shares power, the line managers must change their management behaviour, and the staff take on responsibility that goes beyond their technical tasks. "The purpose of real engagement is to put people at the heart of the change and decision-making process to make change faster and more sustainable" (Smythe 2007). If this succeeds, the organisation will not only be more likely to be successful in implementing the current change process, the company will simultaneously be in an excellent position to launch further change processes: management and staff will be ready for permanent change.

References

Bryant, Lee (2007) Five things to remember when creating your strategy. In: How to use social media to engage employees. Strategies to improve communication and collaboration. Melcrum Publishing, Chicago/London, pp 20–21

Hofstede, Geert (2001) Lokales Denken, globales Handeln. Interkulturelle Zusammenarbeit und globales Management. (2. durchgesehene Auflage) (in German). Deutscher Taschenbuch Verlag (Beck-Wirtschaftsberater), Munich

Insidedge-GolinHarris (2006a) Should I Stay or Should I Go? U.S., U. K. Workers Confirm that Good Communication Fuels Employee Trust and Retention. Press Release Feb 27, 2006, http://www.golinharris.com/pdf/EmployeeSurvey _Insidedge_GolinHarris_and_TOPLINE.PDF (as of: Oct. 2007)

Insidedge-GolinHarris (2006b) Snapshot of US and UK. Insidedge-GolinHarris Employee Communications Survey, http://www.golinharris.com/cap_global_ internal.htm (as of: Oct. 2007)

Kotter, John P. (1996) Leading Change. Harvard Business School Press, Boston

Langen, Ralf (2007) Kommunikation: Soziale Software für erfolgreiches Change Management (in German). In: Communication Agenda. Informationsservice für Kommunikations- und Reputationsmanagement, p. 1, http://www.pleon.de/fileadmin/user_upload/CommAgendaJan2007.pdf. (as of Oct. 2007).

Lotter, Wolf (2007) Elementarteilchen (in German). In: Brandeins, Vol. 9, No. 2: 52–61

McAfee, Andrew P. (2006) Enterprise 2.0: The Dawn of Emergent Collaboration. In: MITSloan Management Review, Vol. 47, No. 3: 21–28

McKinsey (2007) How businesses are using Web 2.0: A McKinsey Global Survey. In: The McKinsey Quarterly, Web exclusive: 1–9, http://www.mckinseyquarterly.com/How_businesses_are_using_Web_20_A_ McKinsey_Global_Survey_1913_abstract (as of: Oct. 2007)

Melcrum (2007) How to use social media to engage employees. Strategies to improve communication and collaboration. Melcrum Publishing, Chicago/London

Moorcroft, David (2006) Realizing RBC's new vision for employee communication. Shifting the goal from informing to engaging. In: Strategic Communication Management, Vol. 10, No. 6: 30–33

O'Reilly, Tim (2005) What Is Web 2.0? Design Patterns and Business Models for the Next Generation of Software. http://www.oreillynet.com/pub/a/oreilly/tim/ news/2005/09/30/what-is-web-20.html (as of: Oct. 2007)

Palmisano, Samuel J. (2004) Leading Change When Business Is Good. In: Harvard Business Review, December: 60–70

PeopleMetrics (2007) Business is Personal: Study Finds Passion and Profits Do Mix.   http://www.people-metrics.com/home/resources/presseereleases_Bis PMay07.htm (as of: Oct. 2007)

Smythe, John (2004a) Engaging people at work to drive strategy and change. Research into how organisations are engaging their leaders and employees in developing strategy and change which points to a growing belief in the value of an inclusive approach. Version 4 non participants.
http://www.engageforchange.com/engagement/articles/index.html (as of: Oct. 2007)

Smythe, John (2004b) Personnel Today 2004. Want to communicate effectively with staff? http://www.engageforchange.com/engagement/articles/index.html (as of: Oct. 2007)

Smythe, John (2007) The CEO: The Chief Engagement Officer. Turning Hierarchy Upside Down to Drive Performance. Gower Publishing Limited, Aldershot

Trebesch, Karsten (2007) Die Beteiligung der Betroffenen in Veränderungsprozessen. Die Unterscheidung der ideologischen und funktionalen Begründungen (in German). In: OrganisationsEntwicklung, No. 3: 31–34

The importance and use of analyses in change management

Rainer Lang and Julia Zangl

More than ever, companies and organisations are subject to a growing pressure to change in order to be able to operate successfully in the long term. As the demands on companies' ability to change has grown, a range of methods and instruments has been developed to support and assist them in their handling of change processes, i.e. in change management.

Instruments that monitor or evaluate the progress and success of the change process are used very rarely. This is confirmed by a survey carried out by the management consultancy Capgemini among corporate executives in Germany, Austria and Switzerland. It concludes that, although the overwhelming majority of executives are acquainted with the instruments for evaluating change processes, they hardly use them in practice. Only 15 percent of the interviewees said they used a Balanced Scorecard in change management; only seven percent used a professional analysis of the corporate culture. Although they agreed that consistent monitoring and controlling of the process should be part of successful change management, only 14 percent of the managers asked were in favour of using change controlling or a Balanced Scorecard in their company (Capgemini 2005).

Scientific literature, too, only gives a rudimentary treatment of the planned, empirical evaluation of change processes – compared to the many publications on change management in general.

Yet many more change processes fail than succeed. The top managers interviewed estimated the likelihood of a change process being a complete success at below 20 percent (Houben et al. 2007). One of the main reasons for the failure of change processes is seen in the lack of consideration given by management to the so-called 'soft factors' (e.g. attitudes and values of the staff) as opposed to the 'hard factors' (e.g. business ratios). Similarly, the implications and effects of the process are frequently underestimated.

Change processes are considered to be failures if the planned changes do not become generally and permanently accepted in the company. Yet the failure of a change process can be effectively counteracted by regular monitoring. Using analyses at the beginning and in the course of the change process is particularly important for its success.

Change controlling

The monitoring or evaluation of a change process is called **change controlling**. A distinction needs to be made here between **process evaluation** and **result evaluation** (Greif et al. 2004). Whereas result evaluation makes a summarising assessment of the change process, process evaluation aims to describe the original situation before and during the change and to monitor individual change steps, so as to form a basis for deriving ways of optimising the ongoing process. Revealing the barriers and drivers of change makes it possible to direct and optimise the change process.

Pure result evaluation is less suitable for monitoring change processes, since a company cannot afford to wait until the end of the project before measuring success. This applies especially to long-term change processes that are usually extremely important to the company. The risk that the desired changes have been only partially realised (or not at all) will be too great. For this reason, at least intermediate results – or better still, individual project steps – must be evaluated and/or monitored. By carrying out continuous measurements as each 'milestone' is reached, changes in direction can be initiated and individual measures corrected and optimised.

Change controlling by process evaluation should therefore be seen as an ongoing cycle in which the implementation of the change process is continuously monitored by comparing planned target figures with the figures that are actually achieved. In practice, the primary aim here is to review individual advances in the change process on the basis of pre-defined values or ratios, in order to build on them to benefit from people's willingness to change and learn in companies.

Only by looking at what change has achieved and making the review a collective process can the process of learning be institutionalised and become part of the 'way we do things around here' (Holbeche 2006).

Different procedures are available for process evaluation during the individual phases of a change process (Table 1).

Table 1. Use of analytical instruments in individual phases of the change process

Phase	Aim	Analytical instrument
Analyse original situation	• analyse market situation • recognise opportunities and risks • analyse willingness to change • identify drivers and barriers	• SWOT analysis • interviews with executives/focus groups • survey of external stakeholders • culture check (zero measurement)
Define targets	• define strategic targets • specify communication aims • formulate vision • formulate mission	
Develop strategy	• formulate "case for change" • develop communication strategy • develop change strategy • organise project management	
Implement changes	• optimise processes • define subprojects • specify milestones • pass on knowledge/skills • create willingness to change • change attitudes and modes of behaviour	• Change Scorecard • feedback systems • focus groups • evaluation of individual measures, events, etc.
Institutionalise changes	• continue/revive change process • communicate successes • develop and encourage staff • consolidate changes in organisation	• Change Scorecard • feedback systems • media response analysis
Cultivate new modes of behaviour	• integrate new behaviour into corporate culture • communicate the relationship between change and corporate success • develop/carry out measures to ensure the sustainability of the change	• survey of external stakeholders • culture check (control measurement)

Change controlling should already be incorporated into planning as specifically as possible in the run-up to a change process. The following aspects should be taken into account in this context (Haiss 2001):

- aims of the measurement (what do we want to achieve with the results?)
- integration of existing data

- timing of the measurement (at the beginning of the change, at individual milestones, final check on success)
- target groups (active people/those involved in the measurement) and their samples (number of interviews)
- survey methodology (qualitative or quantitative)
- client/initiator of the evaluation
- recipient of the evaluation results
- content-related dimensions of the measurement (what is measured?)
- data sources and their reliability (quality criteria: validity, reliability)
- past experience in controlling change processes
- presentation of the results and their use (e.g. discussions)
- deciding further measures
- integration into the change process
- costs

The right choice of observational field, the base period, the measurement parameters, the deviation analysis based on set values, and the assessment of the benefit or effectiveness of changes relative to the original aims – these all represent decisive prerequisites for an effective control and protection of the change process (Haiss 2001).

Demands on the execution of change controlling

The optimal situation is to have an internal or external project team for the execution of change controlling. Both offer advantages. Arguments in favour of an external project team include its greater objectivity and its neutral view of the company. Expert know-how and specialised expertise are more likely to be present in external teams with change experience. An internal team, on the other hand, is more familiar with the specific conditions at the company and the desired change process. Staff are perhaps more likely to trust people they know and who are willing to get involved. However, the risk of using an internal controlling team, especially in the case of evaluation at staff level, is that the input made by the employees may be oriented towards 'socially desired' criteria, and the freedom to express opinions may be limited. This problem emerges in particular when, for example, jobs are threatened or the staff are affected by similarly profound restrictions. In such cases, the anonymity of staff surveys is more likely to be assured by an external project team. However, the related external storage of staff data may be rejected by HR managers or works councils because they would have no control over it.

If the decision is taken in favour of an internal project team, it should not be located at the level of management. Rather, management's key tasks are to create the overall conditions and orientation for monitoring and to make new decisions on the basis of monitoring results. If proposals for adjustment are developed and adopted at the highest level of the hierarchy, this will accelerate and assure their implementation within the change process.

Data protection and other rights certainly have to be taken into account. It is imperative that they are observed to the letter, especially when carrying out staff surveys. The crucial issue here is to respect the rights of the works council. For staff surveys, these can range from the simple right to be informed to codetermination rights or the right to continuous participation, depending on how the survey is designed. Hence, before a staff survey in the context of change controlling is launched, operational questions have to be clarified with the works council in a company agreement.

It is helpful when planning change controlling to have access to existing data – in the case of corporate mergers, to data from both companies. Especially in the case of corporate mergers, this is not always so, because, for example, it might not yet be officially known what company is to be taken over.

Staff and change controlling

The role of the staff within a change process was neglected for a long time, and right up to the 1990s there was a clear division between strategy-directed and staff-centred approaches in change management. Today, however, there is a holistic view of change processes in companies that includes economic, structural aspects and issues of staff psychology. This stems not least from the realisation that the staff make a crucial contribution to the success or failure of a change process. If they are not willing to accept – and also implement – the changes that are asked of them, the desired change cannot be achieved.[1]

One of the key tasks of change controlling is to note the different reactions of the staff, take them seriously and guide them in the desired direction using suitable instruments. This relates primarily to examining and controlling the following factors:

- the communication of information and know-how/knowledge

---

[1] This problem is covered in detail in the contribution by Marit Gerkhardt, Dieter Frey and Peter Fischer in this volume.

- the acceptance of new structures or systems
- the change in motivations, attitudes, basic values and/or the corporate culture

Employees must have all the information they need to implement the change. Furthermore, they must also be willing to implement their know-how in new structures and systems. Because, ultimately, the necessary changes are not just to be carried out once, but internalised and accepted by the staff – i.e. they are supposed to become a part of the corporate culture.

Although these mental factors can be assigned by pressure 'from the top', a long-term, sustainable change primarily needs acceptance at staff level if it is to assert itself in the long term against old habits, structures and attitudes. This requires the involvement of all participants and everyone affected.

The use of change controlling has a double effect on the staff. First, by monitoring the change process, the management is signalling that they mean business and that the process has a long-term orientation. Second, change controlling and related measures, such as staff surveys, generate expectations on the part of the staff regarding the planned changes. Hence, change controlling not only helps monitor the change process, but also contributes towards generating attention and acceptance for change management.

Areas of application for change controlling

The various instruments of change controlling essentially cover not only evaluation methods at the staff level, but also ratio-oriented or feedback-driven approaches. In practice, of course, change controlling monitors more than the process itself: it also evaluates individual measures or instruments of change management. Which individual measures are evaluated will depend, among other things, on how much importance is attached to them in the change process. Table 2 lists some examples of measures, together with appropriate analytical instruments and possible aims of the evaluation.

Table 2. Areas of application of change controlling (examples)

Measure	Analytical instrument	Aims
Intranet; microsites; blogs; digital feedback	Log file analysis; continuous monitoring	Measurement of the frequency of use, observation of opinions, criticism, moods, etc.
Events	Survey of participants (before/afterwards)	Ascertainment of expectations and assessment of the event, perhaps also of the willingness to change
Workshops; training courses; instruction	Survey of participants (before/afterwards)	Analysis of the level of knowledge; communication of information
Press and media relations	Analysis of media response	Analysis of published opinions; monitoring of target-group-specific messages
External communications	Survey of individual stakeholders; external target groups	Monitoring of the communication of information, analysis of the assessment of the change process from outside
Strategy discussion with top managers	Qualitative one-to-one interviews; focus groups	Survey of expectations, identification of possible drivers and barriers in the change process

Evaluation at staff level

Evaluation at staff level primarily involves examining the above-mentioned areas of 'corporate culture', 'information/knowledge transfer' and 'acceptance'.

The analysis of the corporate culture is of key importance here. This '(corporate) culture check' should especially be carried out in the case of takeovers or mergers, since the coming together of different corporate cultures can permanently disrupt the change process. If there are contradictions between the two corporate cultures, then misunderstandings, prejudices and non-acceptance can be expected among the staff.

Since virtually every change process in a company involves a change in the corporate culture, in the context of change controlling, analyses are definitely recommended before (zero measurement), perhaps during, and also after the change process (control measurement). This makes it possible to plan, direct and monitor necessary changes that affect the corporate culture in a more targeted fashion. Hence, the following survey questions are conceivable for a staff analysis within a change process:

- Was everyone affected sufficiently informed, in good time, about the planned changes?
- Did all the necessary information on the change process and the individual measures reach the staff?
- Was all the information understood correctly and in context?
- What attitudes, modes of behaviour, standards and values exist?
- Are the arguments and the information about the change process credible?
- Are the staff given support in implementing the requested changes?
- Does the management stand behind the changes?
- How do the staff judge decision-making in the process?
- Is there not only the ability, but also the willingness to change in the desired direction? (Borg 2003)

Quantitative and qualitative methods

There are various data-collection methods for obtaining the required information. One quantitative method that is still in frequent use is the standardised interview, which is carried out either among all the staff (complete survey) or among a subgroup/grading group (partial survey).

Apart from the quantitative method of the standardised staff survey, another possibility is to use qualitative methods, e.g. manual/theme-based interviews or focus groups. Among other things, these have the advantage that interviewers can answer questions and record additional situation or case-specific information during the survey. Opinions, emotions and motives – i.e. effects at the psychological level – can be recorded more precisely using qualitative methods. The higher creativity potential stimulates ideas, for example on ways to optimise the change process. Structural interrelationships can be uncovered.

However, these qualitative survey methods have the significant disadvantage that only some of the employees can be involved and interviewed. This means that the results cannot be generalised. Furthermore, it is not possible to carry out these methods anonymously, so there is a danger that no usable results are obtained, especially in the context of what is perhaps already an emotionally stressful situation in the midst of a change process. If the overwhelming majority of the staff do not have a positive attitude towards the planned change, and if the company, furthermore, does not cultivate a particularly open communication culture, then very few interviewees will express their opinions openly in interviews or make a constructive contribution to a discussion.

One conceivable possibility is to combine a qualitative interview – covering all aspects of the change process from different perspectives (hierarchy levels) – with a quantitative standardised staff survey in which these aspects are examined on a wide base. One holistic and innovative approach that uses both qualitative and quantitative methods is known as the 'Change Explorer'. It is described in detail towards the end of this contribution.

Online staff surveys are possible in organisations in which all – or at least the great majority of – staff have access to the Internet and/or intranet. There can be time savings and logistical advantages in using an online survey, particularly in companies with a large workforce – which also yields a large sample. Above all, this method makes it possible to take such a 'pulse check' at frequent intervals – and, within certain limits, these results can, in turn, be used as change communication measures themselves.

Feedback systems

Data from staff surveys only becomes useful feedback for companies if they are integrated into improvement processes. When monitoring a change process, it is advisable to question all groups taking part about the progress, and their understanding of the individual change steps and to make their replies part of a uniform feedback mechanism. This feedback system can function in a similar way to the 360° feedback model for assessing executives, for example. The change process is at the centre of the system instead of the executive, and it is judged by all the relevant target groups (staff, executives, managers, project managers, etc.). The change process is then assessed from various perspectives and simultaneously reflected on by participants. The continuous feedback reveals both the drivers and the barriers in the change process and encourages openness to the need for optimisation.

In order to make the final evaluation of the results of the change process, external stakeholder groups could be approached, for example, customers or suppliers – assuming that these are directly affected by the change process. A survey of customers or suppliers could yield an outside assessment of the process, making it possible to include external aspects such as the image or reputation of the company in the evaluation process.[2]

The ratio-oriented approach: The Change Scorecard

The Balanced Scorecard structures a company's financial and non-financial ratios from four perspectives: finance, customers, (internal) processes and innovation/learning. The Balanced Scorecard is always based on a cause/effect correlation, i.e. the cause-and-effect relations between the ratios of the individual perspectives are analysed to make it possible to measure strategic target achievement and to implement the derived necessary measures.

In the context of a change process, the Scorecard approach is suitable for determining the current, actual state of the company and the target state that is desired from individual perspectives. The innovation and learning perspective (also called the staff perspective) is of particular importance in this context; it depicts the ratios relating to the general willingness of the company and its staff to change. Individual processes and workflows – i.e. even the change-controlling process itself – can also be analysed and optimised with the help of this 'Change Scorecard'.

Because it incorporates both monetary and non-monetary perspectives, the Scorecard represents a holistic analytical instrument which also includes the staff and can thus have a positive effect on the acceptance of the change process.

Using a Change Scorecard makes it possible to operationalise, present and communicate a change strategy. It reveals deficits and ideally provides a basis for taking individual measures within the change process. For example, the messages to be communicated can be optimised or adapted to specific target groups.

However, a lot of time and attention needs to be spent on the Scorecard's ratios if these – indeed the best possible – effects are to be guaranteed. The development of these ratios is tied to special demands. They

---

[2] See the contribution by Robert Wreschniok in this volume on the importance of individual reputation factors within a change process.

should be both informative and changeable. The challenge lies in specifying as few ratios as possible which are simultaneously as relevant as possible.

Improving the prospects of success in change – 'Change Explorer'

The so-called 'Change Explorer'[3] is an interview procedure in which change characteristics are analysed using success and failure criteria. It covers subjective assessment characteristics (advantages, disadvantages), the implementation of the planned measures, and the degree of target achievement. Not only quantitative figures, but also qualitative descriptions or expert opinions can be examined for the purposes of assessment.

The aim of this method is to systematically record and describe practical knowledge and assessments using successful changes and failure criteria. The instrument is based on the idea that change projects are not assessed using theoretical knowledge but using practical knowledge that is mostly acquired implicitly. In the practical application of the 'Change Explorer', the interview is supplemented by suitable data from controlling (see Balanced Scorecard) and standardised written surveys for appraising the change. As a rule, these standardised surveys appraise standard characteristics which are generally regarded as important for the success of change processes. They include, for example, the assessment of the project management, the project team, external advisors and available resources, as well as the appraisal of cultural differences and the occurrence of communication problems and conflicts.

As a rule, the manual/theme-based interview is carried out at all management levels. The different opinions, experiences and observations are presented in workshops. The aim is to put together an assessment that is as up-to-date as possible and that can be used as a basis for further measures. This means that, unlike conventional staff surveys, evaluation using the 'Change Explorer' cannot be carried out anonymously. The result is that it can only succeed if management agrees to this way of openly expressing opinions. When it comes to critical projects of corporate policy, however, we recommend carrying out anonymous interviews to ensure that opinions are openly expressed.

---

[3] The 'Change Explorer' was developed at the University of Osnabrueck by the psychologists S. Greif, B. Runde and I. Seeberg. See Greif et al. (2004), pp 325

The 'Change Explorer' can be used both in the course of the change process (process evaluation) and after the change to make a final assessment (result evaluation). In order to be able to recognise failure criteria and reduce failures, it is advisable to include a systematic evaluation in the planning phase of the change process. In the case of continual process evaluation, the 'Change Explorer' should be carried out at each milestone of the project.

Outlook

Companies will see growing pressure to change continuously in the future. This will further increase the importance of change management. 54 percent of the managers interviewed by the management consultants Capgemini believe that change management will be 'important' (42 percent think 'very important') in their company in the future (Capgemini 2005). Furthermore, companies are increasingly demanding change processes that are justified from an economic point of view.

In order to be able to shape, direct and justify the change, you also have to know which direction it is going. However, this can only happen on the basis of continuous monitoring. Change controlling can best make a valuable contribution to change management when the course and progress of the change process are made transparent, and meaningful measures for achieving targets are used. "Measurement systems that show the progress of change, its drivers, barriers and above all the underlying capacity for change, as transparently and communicably as possible can become effective levers that generate pressure to change" (Haiss 2001).

This pressure to change (or the acceptance of changes) is fundamental to the success of the change process. A special form of change controlling supports the change process by defining drivers and barriers within the process and evaluating the effects of individual measures. This makes it possible to take swift countermeasures when results deviate from the targets.

Innovative instruments such as the Change Explorer enable the comprehensive analysis of all relevant aspects from different areas and frequently combine qualitative and quantitative survey methods in the process.

Like all other management fields, change processes require economic legitimisation in the long term. The economic benefit provides proof of the efficiency of a change process and thus supplies arguments for its permanent implementation. Determining the benefits and costs of a change process is important for justifying change measures. The economic benefit of a change process can, however, only be proven by systematic controlling.

Irrespective of whether the effectiveness of a change process is to be justified on the basis of hard or soft factors in each case, systematic analyses are needed to document the 'return on change management'.

References

Borg, Ingwer (2003) Führungsinstrument Mitarbeiterbefragung. Theorien, Tools und Praxiserfahrungen (in German). Hogrefe, Goettingen

Capgemini (2005) Veränderungen erfolgreich gestalten. Change Management 2005. Bedeutung, Strategien, Trends (in German). Capgemini Consulting, Berlin

Elsweiler, Bernd (2002) Erweitertes Monitoring- und Benchmarkingsystem zur strategischen Unternehmenslenkung (in German). Shaker, Aachen

Greif, Siegfried/Runde, Bernd/Seeberg, Ilka (2004) Erfolge und Misserfolge beim Change Management (in German). Hogrefe, Goettingen

Haiss, Peter R. (2001) Monitoring Change. Die Messung von Veränderungsmaßnahmen und -prozessen (in German). In: Gattermeyer, Wolfgang/Al-Ani, Ayad (eds) Change Management und Unternehmenserfolg. Grundlagen, Methoden, Praxisbeispiele. Gabler, Wiesbaden, pp 57–80

Holbeche, Linda (2006) Understanding Change. Theory, Implementation and Success. Elsevier, Oxford

Houben, Anabel/Frigge, Carsten/Trinczek, Rainer/Pongratz, Hans J. (2007) Veränderungen erfolgreich gestalten. Repräsentative Untersuchung über Erfolg und Misserfolg im Veränderungsmanagement. Die wichtigsten Ergebnisse (in German). C4 Consulting GmbH, Duesseldorf

Kraus, Georg/Becker-Kolle, Christel/Fischer, Thomas (2004) Handbuch Change Management. Steuerung von Veränderungsprozessen in Organisationen. Einflussfaktoren und Beteiligte. Konzepte, Instrumente und Methoden (in German). Cornelsen, Berlin

Lammers, Frank (2004) Interview und Fragebogen als Diagnosetechniken (In German). In: Kaune, Axel (ed.) Change Management mit Organisationsentwicklung. Veränderungen erfolgreich durchsetzen. Erich Schmidt, Berlin, pp 88–101

Scherm, Martin/Kaufel, Sven (2005) 360-Grad-Feedback (in German). In: Jöns, Ingela/Bungard, Walter (eds) Feedbackinstrumente im Unternehmen. Grundlagen, Gestaltungshinweise, Erfahrungsberichte. Gabler, Wiesbaden, pp 113–127.

Schewe, Gerhard/Littkemann, Jörn/Schröter, Guido (2004) Kontrolle in Change Management-Prozessen – Mehr als nur Kontrollroutine (in German). In: Bensberg, Frank/vom Brocke, Jan/Schultz, Martin B. (Ed.) Trendberichte zum Controlling. Festschrift für Heinz Lothar Grob. Physica, Heidelberg, pp 111–127.

Zowislo, Natascha/Schwab, Heike (2003) Interne Kommunikation im Verän-
derungsprozess. Mitarbeiter gezielt informieren und erfolgreich einbeziehen
(in German). Gabler, Wiesbaden

Inside

You learn which managers have real leadership skills and which ones constantly make a big deal out of everything.

James Dimon, CEO JP Morgan Chase, 2005–present

The quiet transformation of an ugly duckling: The German Federal Employment Agency's gradual transition – From a bottomless pit for taxpayers' money to an efficient service provider

John-Philip Hammersen

Two numbers that are only indirectly related – five million and eleven billion – mark the biggest reform process a German public authority has ever had to undergo. Five million – this was the almost magical-sounding number of unemployed that was exceeded in early 2005. Although this development did not really surprise any of the experts, it stood for the failure of the Schröder government. And in the eyes of the public, it also stood for the failure of the Federal Employment Agency (Bundesagentur für Arbeit, or BA) to help more people find work. Eleven billion – this was the size of the surplus (in euros) announced by the BA at the end of 2006. This figure proved that it was possible to reform the notoriously cumbersome "mammoth authority" and enable it to succeed.

Between these two extremes lie two years of reform, a process which, although by no means completed, already indicates a transformation from a bottomless pit for taxpayers' money into an efficient organisation, from an unmanageable colossus to a well-structured enterprise. The BA's board of management defined three development phases, starting in 2004, with the aim of turning it into a customer-oriented service provider in the labour market and providing better assistance to people. In the first phase, from 2004 to 2006, the task was to make the BA manageable and transparent. The second phase, which has now begun and will end in 2009, is focusing all efforts on improving operational performance. And the motto of the third phase, which will begin in 2009, is "innovation", because the BA must face up to the challenges of globalisation, demography and the changing world of work.

The BA was in urgent need of reform. To understand this we need to take a brief look back into the past. Virtually complete employment prevailed in Germany up to the mid-nineteen-seventies. The little unemployment there was resulted from the normal and desirable dynamics of the labour market. Structural unemployment began to emerge for the first time after the first oil crisis, rising increasingly higher and higher in a series of waves over the following decades. In January 2005, when people who had previously been on income support were added to the official unemployment statistics following the so-called Hartz Reform, the figure of five million unemployed was exceeded in Germany for the first time since the Second World War.

As the phenomenon of mass unemployment developed, the labour-market authorities also had to keep on expanding. Today the BA has a workforce of more than 100,000, over 800 locations in Germany and an annual budget of over €40 billion. Essentially an insurance enterprise, the BA is bound by numerous laws in its daily work. This is one reason why a typical public-authority structure and culture have developed over the decades. Modern management terms such as controlling, logistics, cost-effective management or customer orientation were largely foreign to the organisation up to the beginning of the reform. The BA was an "enforcement agency" which thought and operated according to laws and tried to fulfil the statutory rights of unemployed people. The BA succeeded neither in efficiently finding work for people, nor in keeping within the budget it was allocated (from paid insurance premiums), so that the federal government had to subsidise it year after year to the tune of billions of euros. Although this was partially due to the overall economic and political climate, the BA was repeatedly criticised in this situation – and in the end fundamentally called into question – by politicians and the public. There was talk of "smashing" it, and it was referred to as the "Colossus of Nuremberg" which was doing nothing but administering unemployment.

This was the situation when Frank-Jürgen Weise took over as chairman of the board of management in the spring of 2004. Looking back, Weise today says: "The BA was a complex restructuring case." This assessment was backed up by a survey carried out by the Allensbach Institute in 2005: only six percent of all Germans still had confidence in the BA. The organisation's public image was terrible. Weise, who had moved to the BA from industry, pursued a consistent course based on five fundamental pillars:

- create transparency
- measure performance
- manage through targets
- decentralise
- aim to be the best

Yet this alone was not enough. The BA also needed an efficient business model. External consultants played a major role in developing and introducing this. Based on the conviction that the BA operates a "mass business", however much it tries to provide individual help, together with the board, these consultants developed the basic framework of a "system business", laying down uniform standards and work processes. The core of this system business in the employment agencies is the "Customer Centre" with its call centre. This will be explained in greater detail below. In order to standardise processes in the work with customers (i.e. job seekers and employers), "action programmes" were introduced defining minimum service standards and giving every member of staff clear guidance on how they can develop future strategies for unemployed people – while also convincing employers of the BA's services.

However, the BA first had to be made manageable. This was primarily made possible through transparency. This was a new word for many areas within the BA. For decades, there had been neither internal nor external transparency on financial flows, the BA's performance or operational efficiency. The result was a highly complex, unmappable structure which simply seemed to soak up billions of euros in insurance premiums and tax money, yet was powerless to combat rising unemployment.

There was thus no alternative but to start the painful process of questioning all work processes and all activities. Surprisingly, the most important tools used in this context came from the fields of controlling and logistics. True to the principle that "you can only control what you can measure", the initial questions that were asked were unusual for a social agency. How long are people unemployed on average? What does that cost? How can we shorten the period of unemployment? What does it cost to integrate an unemployed person into the labour market? How effective are individual labour-market measures? How do the results of certain employment agencies compare to others? Which of BA's services are financed by contributions and which by taxation? Today, all of these questions are monitored and answered within the framework of a strict controlling system. At the same time, the regional and local labour markets in Germany were scientifically analysed and divided into twelve types with comparable conditions. The idea was to be able to realistically compare the performance of the individual employment agencies in an internal system of competition, and this is only possible if the agencies due to be measured share similar characteristics.

Logistics became involved when the focus was on how the BA actually handles its "orders" – admittedly a very technical term given the background of the situations experienced by unemployed people. It was necessary, however, to gain clarity on the nature of the business. Before the reform, the BA worked in the following way: the employment agency's doors were opened in the morning, crowds of people pushed in and picked up a waiting number; when their number was finally called, they explained their problems to a counsellor whose phone was permanently ringing. Under such pressure, there was hardly any time to give qualified advice to help people find a job quickly. The time devoted each customer in such meetings averaged about seven minutes. The aim was therefore to control the flow of customers to free up more time for counselling and to abolish the undignified system of assigning numbers.

The solution that was found was called the Customer Centre, and all former employment offices have successively been converted. Each centre is divided into a reception, an entrance zone, a counselling area and a call centre. Today, 80 percent of all inquiries can be clarified by phone. If a customer needs – or wants – to come to the centre in person, he or she is met in person before actual registration by a BA staff member who can clarify the more simple questions (e.g. notification about vacation dates) immediately. Appointments are made for counselling meetings, for which both sides – BA staff and customers – are then well prepared. Now, an average customer meeting lasts 45 minutes.

Customer centres and action programmes were initially tested intensively in pilot agencies to determine how well they worked in practice and were then successively introduced within a year in the 178 employment agencies nationwide in nine phases. The agencies and their management teams were given intensive support by internal advisory teams from the BA's central office. All members of staff were given training at the BA's own training centres to enable them to get to know and understand the new work sequences. This was not all, however. Important software systems also had to be replaced by modern successors at the same time – a Herculean task, since the BA operates 150,000 PCs nationwide and every program has to be specially developed to carry out the BA's specialised tasks.

The introduction of customer centres, action programmes and software was constantly monitored in a control centre at the BA central office. Notice boards in the control centre provide a constant, quick overview of the progress of planning, implementation and monitoring of the respective projects. One system that has proved useful assesses every process step using little traffic lights in the unequivocal colours of red, amber and green. The traffic lights make it immediately evident where adjustments or interventions are necessary. However, this only gives an internal view of the BA. In order to also obtain an external perspective on its reform progress, the BA conducts regular customer surveys among both job seekers and employers to assess the degree of customer satisfaction with the agency. All employment agencies have been given clear targets on when customer satisfaction must improve to what level. The satisfaction level of staff is determined in surveys in order that problems or dissatisfaction with individual reform elements can be recognised and solved.

The results of the surveys show an encouraging development. Today, employers and job seekers are significantly more satisfied with the service provided by the BA; the friendliness of the staff in particular is praised, which shows that the service principle has largely become established. Similarly, the satisfaction of staff with their work and their employer has been improving since the beginning of the reform on several important points, although some people have become "tired" with reforms. After all, the individual reform projects have meant substantial changes and burden for the staff. Eighty percent of all work processes have been changed. Furthermore, these changes had to be dictated "from above", i.e. by the board of management, since there was no time for a lengthy democratic process in the organisation. This has caused friction, of course. Yet, since the BA is a very hierarchical organisation in the tradition of German public authorities, most colleagues soon began to appreciate the freedoms which the new management system gave them: today, the agencies set their own targets, are responsible for reaching these targets, and have accordingly also been given greater discretionary powers and scope for decision-making. Also, the improvement in customer flows and the fact that they have more time for customer meetings have convinced most of the BA staff.

In 2005, the new work sequences in operational business and management brought clarity on financial flows and the effect of the funds used for the first time in the BA's history. The individual employment agencies were compared for the first time. Problematic issues were discussed in all openness within the BA leadership – again for the first time. Not all the conclusions were encouraging. So how could the public perception of the organisation be improved? The answer was, again, to launch a transparency offensive. Up to this time, the BA's public-relations work had tended to be defensive, reactive and mindful of "keeping the lid on" certain issues. Essentially, active press work began and ended with the monthly publication of labour-market data. The organisation was uncertain on how to handle the media and rarely had the courage to go on the offensive. However, since the BA – the largest public authority in Germany, administering a budget worth billions and with a mandate to fight the most urgent of social problems – was always in the public focus, information was constantly seeping out of the organisation into the public domain via informal channels. This resulted in reports full of speculation and conjecture. The BA, as a result, increasingly became an object – and, some people said, a victim – of reporting, without effectively intervening in the media game itself.

This had to be changed. Today, the BA actively goes public on relevant issues, be they positive or negative. In this way, it at least maintains sovereignty over interpretation and limits "wild research" by journalists among its staff. The BA always responds to on every query, irrespective of how critical it might be. The BA often used to make "no comment" which could hardly have had a worse effect on public opinion; this is no longer the case. The BA's press offices (each agency has a spokesperson) regard the media as partners, not as their natural enemy. In concrete terms, this means that the BA answers enquiries quickly, comprehensively, openly, honestly and without prevarication. This has generated respect in the editorial offices, with the result being that today the BA is treated fairly on difficult topics, i.e. it is at least given a chance to make a statement. This was certainly not always the case in the past.

There was no alternative to completely opening up to the media. First, such a large organisation cannot be made "watertight". Information will always get out through one channel or another, be it via personal contacts or Internet forums. Second, Germany has a "freedom of information" act which forces public authorities to publish practically all internal information when an enquiry is made. This law alone makes all blockade tactics futile. Third, it is always a good idea to make it as easy as possible for journalists to do their work. Editorial offices are under immense time pressure these days. Like other companies, publishing houses and radio/TV stations have been cutting costs and laying off staff. Fewer and fewer editors with less and less experience have to serve a news market that is becoming faster all the time. Who won't be grateful for a genuine press office that makes your work easier rather than more difficult? Powerful allies in the media can be won in this way.

However, transparency alone was not enough. The media positioning of the chairman of the board was just as important. This has nothing to do with vanity. Every enterprise needs a figurehead, a publicly visible leadership personality who provides orientation and lays down values, credibly representing key issues like transparency to the outside world. The public find it much easier to develop confidence (or mistrust) in a person than in an institution. This is one reason why the media like to tie their stories to people; this tendency is stronger, the more complicated the product or service or enterprise is. And the BA is very complicated. Journalists also want to be acquainted with the responsible people; they want to develop a feeling for the kind of person they are dealing with – not only to pass on this picture to their readers/viewers/listeners, but also to find out for themselves whether this person is credible. Can she or he be trusted? Only if journalists are convinced will they begin to believe the enterprise concerned. And only then can a board chairman – and hence the enterprise – successfully get a message across to the public.

The measures taken by the BA to position the board chairman have nothing to do with wizardry. But they do take time. Three tools are essential: interviews/press conferences, background meetings with journalists and visits to editorial offices. The board chairman met well over 150 journalists at such events in 2006 alone. From the BA's point of view, these meetings are not only helpful for explaining the labour market, some aspects of which are very complex, they also enable the media representatives to get to know the chairman better personally. The credibility that can be gained in this way cannot be overestimated.

This was shown after mid-2006. Driven by a reviving economy, the labour market began developing in a surprisingly positive way from month to month. In November, the unemployment figures fell below the four-million mark for the first time in years. The direct consequence was that the BA's finances improved

- since expenditure on unemployment fell and revenue rose with an increase in the number of contributors and
- because the more economical use of funds at the BA began to bear fruit.

The board chairman was given direct credit for this "miracle of Nuremberg" and publicly praised. It would have been easy for the media to ignore the BA's role and focus on the improved overall economic conditions as the sole cause. Yet, since the chairman had a high credibility level, having held numerous personal meetings with journalists and cooperated professionally with the media, his arguments were heard, i.e. that it

- was the BA's reforms – above all values such as transparency – that had made this success possible and ensured that the money did not immediately disappear into obscure channels,
- is right to invest money only if it really helps people,
- is right to organise all work processes in such a way that there is more time for one-to-one meetings with customers, thus improving the chances of people finding a new job.

Therefore, the consequences of the surplus were also credited to the BA's chairman and thus to the organisation:

- As a result of the surplus in 2006, the BA was able to significantly lower the contributions to unemployment insurance (from 6.5 percent to 4.2 percent of wages) for the first time since reunification, thus helping to cut the oppressively high non-wage labour costs.

- The BA will be able to keep this rate of contribution stable up until 2010, making it the only social insurance organisation in Germany that has its finances under control.

In the second, currently ongoing phase of the reform there are two main issues. On one hand, the BA has to prove and *demonstrate* that its improved structures and processes are delivering better assistance to (unemployed) people and that this is more useful to companies (looking for staff) than before. On the other hand, the process of transferring the chairman's positive image to the enterprise as a whole must continue. The BA has set itself the aim of being the most important and best service provider in the German labour market. And this is also how it wants to be perceived by the public. When people come to the employment agency at a difficult time in their lives, it wants to give them the feeling that they really are being helped. And employers must be confident that their concerns and needs are understood by the employment agency. The BA still has quite a long way to go.

How to develop a strategic business unit within a historical and sound structure: The formation of Radeberger Group

Ulrich Kallmeyer

With more than 22,000 employees, the Oetker Group is one of the largest internationally-oriented privately-owned companies in Germany. The company's history is strongly tied to the clear business principles of the owning family. First, the interests of the group take priority over those of the owning family. Second, the Oetker Group banks on self-financed growth with a strict diversification strategy in order to compensate risks within the group: all four core business units conduct their operational business independently. This article describes how 'beer and alcohol-free beverages' developed into one of these core business segments. It also explains the directly-related creation of the Radeberger Group, which saw 14 brewery locations and more than 70 active brands combine into Germany's largest private brewery group. The delicate balance between change and consistency as well as the compensation of risks within the group had the highest priority.

"The interests of the business have priority over those of the family." With this fundamental commitment, the owning family of the Dr. August Oetker KG established the basis for a stable and continuous development of its business. One of the key effects, based on a high ratio of retained earnings and a sustainable as well as healthy profitability, is the group's ability to finance growth out of its own resources. The Oetker Group never targets short-term economic success but pursues long-term prosperity and continuity. This, together with further attributes of the Oetker Group (such as stockholders' structure, the flexibility of the legal form of the private partnership, the significant continuity in key management positions, the internal coherence of the firm and the high identification of the employees with the family business), contributes to the firm's success.

A brief look back

Under the corporate umbrella of the Oetker Group, the businesses of the four strategic divisions develop and expand independently. Today, the firm focuses primarily on the four divisions 'Shipping', 'Food', 'Beer and Non-Alcoholic Beverages' and 'Sparkling Wine, Wine and Spirits'. The present structure of the firm is the result of the maxim once held by Rudolf-August Oetker: "Don't put all eggs into one basket." However, the groundwork for today's success was laid in 1891 when the founder of the Oetker Group, Dr. August Oetker, portioned baking powder into small marketable units and gave his personal guarantee of baking success by branding the product with his name. This was the birth of one of the very first German brands. It is still being marketed today. In the following years, after the challenging post-war period, Dr. Richard Kaselowsky, who had married into the Oetker family, began to intensify advertising, and expanded the firm's businesses into international markets. The founder's grandson, Rudolf-August Oetker, took the lead and rebuilt the firm after World War Two. He continued the internationalisation of the firm, but first focused its on shipping and foodstuffs. Later, the two other strategic divisions were established. Today, Dr. h.c. August Oetker chairs the Oetker Group. His major initiatives have been to sell off non-core businesses, and to streamline and expand the strategic divisions, both nationally and internationally.

Paradigms as the solid foundation of all business decisions

Although the firm's organisational structure has changed over the past century, the same core paradigms shape overall business decisions. First, the interests of the business have priority over those of the family. Second, the firm diversifies and spreads its risks within its entrepreneurial engagements. This is most important, since the core businesses are each influenced by their own individual risks. Third, the operational business of each division is managed locally.

Radeberger Group as a new strategic business unit

With its shipping division booming, the Oetker Group decided to invest into other businesses in order to reduce risks. The decision was made in 2001, and saw the Radeberger Group become a strategic business unit of the Oetker Group. The beer industry attracted the attention of the management board and market leadership became a new prospect for the former Binding-Brauerei AG. Accordingly, the division acquired the Brau und Brunnen AG – the largest investment in the history of the Oetker Group. This acquisition was followed by further investments leading to market leadership with currently 15 percent of all German beer sales (Fig. 1).

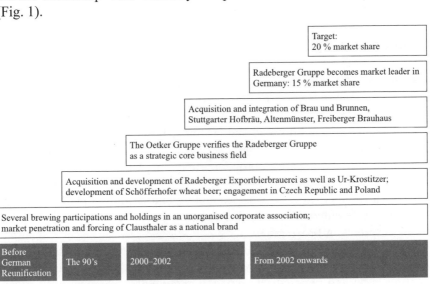

Fig. 1. Acquisition milestones

Today, the company is targeting a market share of at least 20 percent through organic growth and is thus prepared for further acquisitions that will strengthen its market position. Market leadership and consumer oriented brand and product management are crucial in order to have a significant impact on the beer market. Thanks to the changes described below, the company (with its diversified portfolio and positioning) fills these important success criteria in the German beer market. In particular, the number and diversity of regional brands prove Radeberger Group's ability to successfully manage both national and local beer brands, and therefore be close to its customers. It is also accompanied by a competitive cost structure. Hence, not only the brand management but also the strategic management follows the three core beliefs:

1. Beer needs a homeland.
2. Beer needs brand awareness.
3. Beer needs profitability.

With this in mind, the Radeberger Group is able to compete not only in terms of beer sales, but in achieving financial goals, which are necessary in order to capitalise on external growth opportunities. Altogether, the beer and non-alcoholic division of the Oetker Group has successfully managed (and continues to manage successfully) a major transformation process and demonstrates its role as a core business field within the family business.

Change in progress

This period of acquisitions put the emerging Radeberger Group in a situation of continuous change. Following the formal merger of the previously independent breweries, the newly established organisation focused on strengthening its overall brand and customer orientation. One of the major challenges in achieving this objective was switching from a traditional hierarchical thinking towards a process orientation. Changing the established workflows and processes at the various locations involved a major process of reorganisation. The goal was a common and definitive market orientation, i.e. differentiated and distinguishable products that increase brand value despite their broad range.

Today, all brands of the national portfolio are strategically administered centrally and operationally managed at regional level. The combination of centralisation and regionalisation of the operational sequences streamlines processes and reduces diversity at consumer level. Following a holistic approach towards the change process, the remaining divisions were centralised and arranged in a process-orientated way as well. The only exception with respect to distribution channels is the sales structure, which needs to be decentralised due to the importance of regional markets. The reorganisation aimed for national, homogeneous market penetration via differentiated brand management. At the same time, it aimed to realise cost synergies and hasten the integration of the acquired businesses. However, there was the crucial challenge of implementing a consistent corporate philosophy throughout the group. Company-wide meetings and workshops fostered the acceptance of the new corporate values. Certainly, an important asset was, and still is, the commitment on the part of the management to act as role models for these values, symbolically reinforced by the manifesto of the new Radeberger Group (Fig. 2).

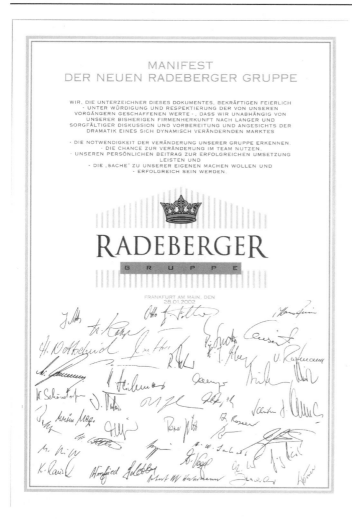

Fig. 2. Manifesto of the new Radeberger Group[1]

---

[1] "We, the signatories of this document, affirm solemnly – under appreciation and respect of the values created by our predecessors – that we independently of our firm origin, after long and careful discussion and preparation and in view of the dramatic of a dynamically changing market: recognise the necessity for change of our group, will take jointly the chance for changes, will carry out our personal contribution for the successful conversion, will make "the thing" our own and will be successful. Frankfurt on the Main, January 28th, 2002". (signed by the 22 leading managers and key players of the change process).

Additionally, the value proposition of the different locations was strengthened by the importance and potential of the various regional brands, as these reflected the ideology of 'beer needs a homeland'. In turn, this regional focus tied in with the group's commitment to a specifically German beer culture.

The beginning: Bringing it all together

In 2000, the Binding Brauerei AG comprised six interdependently operating breweries and one spring for mineral water – each with an individual sales force and administration. Apart from an unfavourable cost structure, it turned out that the strong regional competition between these breweries, which in fact belong to the same company, was more destructive than constructive and profitable. To stop this 'cannibalisation', the objective after the takeover was to adjust the counteractive individual targets of the breweries, and to bring together the seven firms into one administration and one sales force.

Change chronology

The reorganisation of the brewery Dortmunder Actien Brauerei (DAB) was completed ahead of the original schedule. In early 2001, a local change management team was placed on site in order to implement the change according to the overall integration plan. The reorganisation was planned as a five-phase process: The **preparatory phase** started in the beginning of 2002 with the executive committee's and supervisory board's mutual decision to launch an extensive restructuring process. Two project groups – each consisting of selected top management and a small number of external consultants – were set up to develop the future structure of the new organisation. The **second phase** dealt with the identification and definition of core business processes, including a detailed examination and assessment of the product range as well as all business processes. In the **third phase** the core business processes were used to define an 'ideal scenario', which from then on was set as the objective to be achieved. The **fourth phase** was dedicated to the development of a change master plan that defined the milestones, the technical and human resources needed and the timing. Since the approval of this master plan in July 2002, the Radeberger Group has been in the **fifth phase** – a state of continuous change and transformation. The individual sub-projects were realised by project teams that strongly involved the top performers in order to keep them and their know-how within the company. The implementation of the general reorganisation was completed in 2005. Though most of the goals were reached, some tasks will still take some time.

During the reorganisation of the Binding Brauerei AG into the Radeberger Group, additional business opportunities challenged the emerging Radeberger Group and its staff: specifically, there was the takeover of two regional breweries as well as the acquisition of the Brau und Brunnen AG with its seven breweries in 2004. At this point, the Radeberger Group was not yet fully reorganised yet. But the opportunity to acquire the Brau und Brunnen AG made swift integration imperative. In addition to the ongoing change processes, the fact that the publicly traded Brau und Brunnen AG was not in full ownership of the Radeberger Group challenged every player in the process even more. Even though one of the primary aims was to keep as many people as possible with the company, two breweries had to be closed and their entire administration and sales force consolidated. Especially leading up to the integration and the brewery closures, it was important to explain why these steps were necessary. In two cases, all resources had to be concentrated on individual plants in order to secure the site and to safeguard jobs.

In the context of the realignment/reorganisation of the Radeberger Group, the formerly independent breweries were merged into the firm in different ways. The subsidiary Berliner Kindl AG followed a transfer of shares from the minority shareholders to the Binding Brauerei AG. In the case of the Dortmunder Actien Brauerei and Binding Brauerei AG a control and profit-transfer agreement was signed.

For the purpose of better market perception and identification, the name of Binding Brauerei AG was changed into Radeberger Group AG. The large breweries within the group were converted into cost centres, which hold the responsibility for production, logistics, operation and local administration. The sales and distribution department was organised and led as a profit centre with regional sales responsibility.

The human factor: Involvement by communication

The human factor was a central success factor in the change project. Hence, it was important that everybody involved was aware of the corporate culture of the newly designed organisation and felt committed to the venture. All employees had to decide for themselves whether they wanted to accept the challenges and the tasks and responsibilities involved in this common enterprise. This decision could not – and never can – be made by one's supervisor. Once committed, every team member has to assume responsibility for his/her part and yes, sooner or later people will slip up. However, when making mistakes, responsibility demands that one deals openly with them. Organisations and their staff can only learn from them if they are not stifled. Giving confidence and living up to one's own responsibility has much to do with honesty and trustworthiness. The Radeberger Group sustains its commitment to clarity, even when decisions need to be revised. Upcoming tasks and answers to open questions are to be met with

- modesty (with self-confidence, with determination, but without personal vanities and without arrogance),
- passion (paired with friendliness) and
- competence (as a sign of the firm's self-perception).

This is even more important, since, as the project proceeded, more staff got directly involved with the change process via sub-projects. Reorganisation began to affect them and their personal situation. Increasingly, the executive committee delegated responsibilities to the management, which in turn passed on operational responsibility to their staff. This degree of involvement facilitated the utilisation of individual strengths more efficiently and in a more self-determined way. As a result, all team members were treated equally, even in teams that had encountered friction in the past. Instead of disciplinary, authoritarian direction, the leadership of employees was now called for to follow objectives in the context of the restructuring. Furthermore, each individual employee was actively involved in the reorganisation of the new enterprise. Though the policy of 'leading by objectives' was not present in all breweries, discrepancies did arise during its implementation in the group. Thus, the staff had to become familiar with the new requirements and a new working culture.

As a safeguard for active support and cooperation throughout the organisation, a comprehensive internal communications network was implemented. Broad information flows and an explicit readiness for discussion paired with a readiness to solve conflicts within the company ensure constant communication. The development of the migration process was charted in a public data file in "Microsoft Exchange". Furthermore, the executive committee frequently informed project group managers and works councils, who both worked as multipliers. Accordingly, reactions and suggestions from the staff were forwarded to the management. The further the project advanced, the more people were directly involved and thus directly informed. Furthermore, the corporate newspaper and workshop meetings were used to communicate the progress of the migration process. For the organisation of communication within the group, electronic data processing (EDP) systems were vital for the entire process flow. Uniform EDP for the group was a necessary conversion basis for the creation of a new inter-laced organisation. However, EDP was previously different in each enter-prise, and standardising it across the group was a complicated and lengthy process.

Conflicts, hidden agendas and resistance

In the first months of the process, basic conflicts already arose about the need for the reorganisation of the company per se. The general approach was discussed as well, enforced by the varying level of technological knowledge and backgrounds. Apart from criticism of the change in the course of the project, the organisation encountered acts of defiance, which were often a vent for deep-seated personal resistances. Most of the time, the deeper causes of these individual resistances were a dread of new, more complex tasks or a lack of soft – and sometimes hard – skills. A spe-cific form of resistance was to be found at the top management of the re-gional enterprises, as they tried to preserve their position, power and influ-ence. This conflicted with the new philosophy. In many cases these resistances could be resolved via proactive conflict management and an open discussion.

At an early stage of the project, the economic situation was transpar-ently communicated in order to convince everyone of the necessity of the transition and to dissolve resistance and fears – as opposed to breaking it. It also illustrated the individual duties and opportunities that the project presented for everyone. A high identification of the staff with the project and its initiators does help to prevent resistance. Therefore, the change process was moved forward only as fast as the co-workers could manage. If, however, individual privileges needed to be limited, or the situation of an individual co-worker needed to be changed, resistance often could not be avoided, resulting in a loss of mutual understanding. In the case of some local management, disciplinary and functional responsibilities had to be cut. Some layoffs were inevitable.

Conclusion

The management of the change process regulated the interaction of all in-volved participants and processes of the Radeberger Group, and aligned them towards a common goal. The all-encompassing organisational change aimed to increase the flexibility of the organisation in order to cope with a dynamic market. The management identified the underlying principles and challenges for success: beer needs regional reference and brand awareness. However, to be profitable, a market leader has to follow certain rules, set by national and international competitors, but also by an innovative approach to future market scenarios. As a result, an organisation emerged with the highest degree of centralised steering and support possible while taking into account regional business-related issues, which are – at least today – a crucial success factor on a national market with almost 1,300 breweries. Though market structures will change in the future, they are unlikely to reach the oligarchic proportions common on international markets. Be that as it may, the Radeberger Group should cope with a market which develops along the path currently taken.

Managing complex change: Challenges at the National Health Service Greater Glasgow and Clyde

Nic Beech and Robert MacIntosh

When managing change, effective communication is fundamental to success. Indeed, many failures of change initiatives are attributed, in whole or in part, to communication failures (Kotter and Cohen 2002). We have spent the last two years studying an organisation that faced a particularly difficult change challenge. The study reveals some interesting insights. The National Health Service (NHS) Greater Glasgow and Clyde faced a difficult task in that the organisation had a large and change-fatigued group of employees, needed to effect the change very quickly and faced real public scrutiny over the both the change process and performance outcomes. This article explores some of the lessons learnt from this longitudinal and in-depth study of complex, rapid and radical organisational change.

The National Health Service was introduced in the UK in 1948 with the objective of offering healthcare services which were free at the point of delivery; it has since grown to become the third largest employer in the world. Although the NHS is often talked about as a singular organisation, it is in fact made up of many, many components. The advent of devolution meant that responsibility for policy decisions was devolved from the UK's central government to the Scottish Parliament and the Welsh Assembly on their formation in 1999.

NHS Greater Glasgow and Clyde (NHS GG&C) is the largest Scottish health board by some distance and employs around 44,000 staff to provide healthcare to a population of approximately 1.2 million. Partly because of its size, an earlier incarnation of the organisation had been broken up into four autonomous trusts during a previous restructuring. In 2004, the Scottish Executive decided to re-integrate these four organisations into a single pan-Glasgow organisation. Many of the staff involved had therefore lived through several rounds of reorganisation to stitch together or pull apart similar, but distinct, organisational forms. Suffice it to say that staff were not overly enthusiastic about the prospect of another wave of reform.

Here, then, was a huge organisation, facing a complex reorganisation within a very tight time frame. The new organisation had to be up and running within 16 months. Further complication was added several months into the change process when the Government Health Minister took the radical decision to dissolve a neighbouring health board (NHS Argyle and Clyde) which had been posting heavy financial losses for some time. NHS Greater Glasgow, as it was then known, was invited to take on a large geographic territory and the staffing which went with it to form the newly merged NHS Greater Glasgow and Clyde. When questioned about this, the chairman of NHS GG&C said that incorporating 9,000 new staff during an already complicated restructure was "modular". The reality was a little more complex, not least because of the £30 million deficit that was inherited and the demoralised group of staff who had been stigmatised as working for a "failing organisation".

Our interest in studying this particular reorganisation was heightened in early discussions when we realised that there were several other unusual dynamics in play. First, amongst the 44,000 members of staff involved, there are huge disparities in pay, from those on the national minimum wage to a limited number of senior clinicians earning substantial sums. Second, the organisation spans over 80 professional groupings and the NHS as a whole is characterised by a number of intra- and inter-professional rivalries. Within the clinical staff we met senior consultants who claimed: "I'm in more regular contact with research colleagues around the world than I am with people from [hospital name] two miles down the road, and we work for the same organisation."

More problematic still is the somewhat uncomfortable relationship between the clinical staff and the managers. One board member commented that "many of our staff would see 'management' as an entirely negative construct", and other research in the health service highlights the negative views that clinicians hold of managers, who are described as having "started out as office boys" (Lewellyn 2001). A third dynamic is the highly politicised nature of the organisation's work. Both as a large employer and as a provider of vital public services, NHS GG&C is under public scrutiny at all times. This is the first organisation we have met where board meetings take place in public with journalists in attendance. This becomes particularly relevant when you consider the range of national targets for reducing patient waiting times, decreasing health inequalities and so on. Any boardroom discussion has the capacity to become national news and this adds a degree of pressure that is unusual.

Finally, the organisation relies on a large number of partnerships and external contractor arrangements for the delivery of its services in ways which are not necessarily visible to users of those services. A local General Practitioner surgery is in effect an independent trader who is contracted by the health board to provide services, but for the patient it all feels like part of "the NHS". Similarly, the introduction of a new way of working in primary and community-oriented health: Community Health Partnerships, which entailed partnerships between health and other services such as social work, meant that new organisational forms were being developed to deliver joint services with several distinct local authorities in NHS GG&C's territory. Figuring out an effective system of organisational and clinical governance arrangements was a labyrinthine task.

To their credit, those on the management team recognised the scale of the challenge facing them. They saw an opportunity to "reform the NHS in Greater Glasgow and Clyde" and were keen that the change process delivered more than just a reorganisation of reporting lines on an organogram. A set of transformational themes were developed to help ensure that the change process went to the heart of the way NHS GG&C worked (see Table 1). These themes cover issues such as performance and accountability but also leadership and integration with other agencies and services.

Table 1. The Nine Transformational Themes for NHS GG&C

1	Achieving an organisation in which the component parts work together to shared aspirations and objectives, not competing ones, and managers and clinical leaders work in teams with shared values and priorities.
2	The senior team and organisation contribute to leadership on health improvement and tackling inequalities.
3	Focusing on service improvement and equipping and supporting frontline staff and first line managers to help us deliver it.
4	Moving away from functional systems of management to general management with managers at all levels responsible for the quality of service delivered to patients and professional staff developed into management and leadership roles.
5	An organisation where people take responsibility for their area of work and for the wider performance of the organisation.
6	An organisation focused on learning and development, as individuals and collectively, to improve our performance.
7	A culture of clear objectives, accountability and performance management at all levels.
8	Driving integration of acute and community and health and social care services to improve the experience of patients.
9	Leaders and managers who have a value base of public services, acting in the interests of patients and the communities we service, and behave in a collaborative not competitive way but constructively challenge each other.

The complicated nature of organisational life

NHS GG&C employs staff who have different skill sets, attitudes and functions. This is important, as an organisation of clones may not have sufficient diversity to be creative and to effectively fulfil the requirements of specialised functional areas (Herrmann and Datta 2005). There are staff of different ages, and staff focused on different parts of the service. Hence, we should expect there to be differences in opinion and perception.

People perceive things as they impact upon themselves, and hence, what might be a revolutionary change for some, might be unimportant for others. Many organisations are made up of 'competing' views of what is really important, and NHS GG&C is no different. For some employees, for example those working in non-hospital care, the changes were to be dramatic. They would work in new teams, for example, with social workers, and would be managed in new ways. For others, for example some of the professionals in hospitals, although the change would impact on them in time, it was possible to dismiss the change as being 'just another reorganisation' that would not affect day-to-day functioning. Hence, the communication task was accentuated as the change was perceived quite differently by different groups. A central task of leadership is to manage the negotiated understanding of the why, the what and the how of change, and in these circumstances, this task is particularly challenging.

The research process

For over two years, we have had privileged access to the organisation's inner workings. We have been able to attend over 40 regular meetings that senior managers convene (e.g. board meetings, organisational development meetings etc.), we have conducted a series of 46 one-to-one interviews with executive and non-executive directors throughout the process to check the evolution of their thinking, we have held nine focus groups, sent questionnaires to over 500 employees and been given the remit to follow up on lines of inquiry that we saw as relevant. What follows are our analysis and observations about the process of change to date, with the recognition that it is, of course, still taking place.

The need for speed

Faced with such an enormous change, you have two choices. Option A is to carefully analyse the change, to develop carefully thought out proposals and to take your time over the difficult decisions. Option B is to get down to business as quickly as possible. Management consultant Tom Peters once observed that significant organisational change takes place over a weekend or not at all. NHS GG&C did not quite manage the change process over a weekend, though there were a number of crunch weekend sessions to progress key items of business. Still, 14 months from inception to going live was impressive given the complexities set out in the introduction.

The change journey started with consultations about the right structural approach. The need for open consultation seemed obvious and there were several big set-piece meetings attended by the top few hundred managers, as well as several smaller and more focused gatherings. During the consultation process, one audience member noted that he had "never seen this done before because every organisational building block is losing its stability at the same time". At the same meeting, another commented that "this will be my sixth major restructuring in 14 years". Consultation is a time-consuming business and can seem unrewarding. When the Chief Executive was asked in a public forum, "How much of these proposed new structures can we discuss with colleagues?" he answered emphatically, "All of it." Nevertheless, subsequent one-to-one interviews showed that some professional groups, notably the clinicians, felt that they were not being consulted.

As views of the appropriate structure firmed up, the next obvious challenge was developing a robust process for appointing people to roles within the new organisation. Bearing in mind that for most senior posts (e.g. HR director, Finance Director etc.) there were four displaced candidates from the four trusts which were being merged and only one post, this was always going to be a contentious issue. The organisation took the view that some form of assessment centre offered the best means of

- ensuring that the right people with the right skills ended up in the right roles, and
- making the process as equitable and evidence-based as possible. This said, there was also an emphasis on getting it roughly right quickly, rather than absolutely right too late.

In total, almost four hundred candidates were placed into over 300 hundred senior management positions within a period of eighteen months. The process was by no means perfect but what struck us was the relatively small number of controversial decisions. The focus was on getting the competencies required to run the new organisation right from the outset and the assessment centre offered a means of achieving this outcome. The willingness of well qualified, experienced and senior staff, in some cases with 20 or 30 years' experience in the organisation, to participate in the assessment centre process was a significant marker. One senior and experienced candidate said that the assessment centre was "a different process for very many of [us] senior folk".

Achieving the right balance of internal and external expertise

NHS GG&C did have HR and OD experts at its disposal. For reasons of capacity or due to a lack of expertise in specific areas, the organisation did, however, engage external consultants. Finding the right balance between internal resources and outside help was critical. The evident complexities of the organisation, its culture and the sensitivities around the demarcation between different professional groupings made it a very difficult setting for external consultants to achieve credibility. Therefore, most tasks had to be led or overseen by someone from within the organisation. It was not possible, for example, to sub-contract the development of the assessment centre process completely. The counterargument, however, was that it was equally important to recognise the limits of one's own expertise. The notion of a "plucky amateur, helping out in their lunch hour" was not tenable. Professional guidance was sought where it was required, but usually in the context of a partnership agreement that allowed the right blend of local knowledge and outside expertise. This was all the more important given that the world did not stop turning whilst the reorganisation went ahead. Rather, the tricky business of running a high profile organisation continued amid public scrutiny of the process of changing it. Elsewhere, this has been described as the dual tensions of the "organisation of production" and the "production of organisation" (MacIntosh and Romme 2004).

Paying the communication and consultation tax

Most research on change arrives at the conclusion that communication is vital. John Kotter argues that most change programmes fail because they "undercommunicate by a factor of 10" (Kotter 1995). In this case, significant effort went into the attempts to communicate the reasons for the change and the merits of the proposed organisational arrangements. From meeting individuals and clinical groups, to talking with community representatives and arranging public consultation meetings, the Chief Executive of NHS GG&C put an enormous amount of time into the attempt to engage key stakeholders. Not everyone was enthusiastic and there were many, many detailed questions that had to be dealt with or followed up. This was an exhausting process for those individuals centrally involved, particularly when placed on top of demands to continue to perform their day jobs.

In fact, the communication and consultation burden rested very heavily on a limited number of key individuals. "[We] were reflecting on this last week. I think at some key points in the development of this there were probably too few members of my senior team out there selling this, meeting groups of staff, talking them through it. That became a very big task when [name of colleague] and I were meeting 30 [name of staff grouping] not once but twice, three times, with seven rounds of meetings with the senior clinical staff at [name of hospital] to talk through the implications of moving toward more community based services." Perhaps something more could have been done to share this burden more evenly amongst board members. In practice though, these were very delicate discussions where both the consultants and the consultees felt that it was necessary to speak with the most senior management team members. If nothing can be done to change the need for seniority and gravitas in those conversations, more could have been done to ease the burden of the day job. Astute delegation of key tasks during this critical phase, which lasted only a few months, is essential if the communication and consultation tax is not to take too heavy a toll.

Learning lessons across the public-private sector divide

About six months after the new organisational arrangements were put into place, we hosted a research seminar with participants drawn from the boards of two other major public sector organisations and two FTSE-listed companies. The intention of the event was to help the senior management team in NHS GG&C think through the challenges ahead in the change process. Perhaps, the unspoken assumption was that lessons could be learned from the private sector.

This process of external comparison highlighted some interesting points. First, NHS GG&C had achieved a great deal in very difficult circumstances. A board member for one of the private sector firms commented that this was all the more impressive because "politics runs through everything [you do] ... with a big and a little P". Both private sector firms indicated that equivalent processes internally would have produced far higher levels of turnover in staff, either through redundancies or through "performance managing people out of the business". Both private sector firms could point to evidence that staff "regarded the business as being run by management, not the unions, and that no one will tolerate being managed by someone who isn't up to the job". In contrast, those with long experience of the NHS were troubled by the fact that it still felt like the organisation was run by the doctors for the doctors, and that no one would think to ask whether they were being managed, let alone whether they were being managed well. Most strikingly, all five organisations represented at the seminar reported that the opportunity to calibrate their own progress against that of others was hugely valuable. Though each organisation faced very different environments and challenges, each was facing similar problems and each had excelled in slightly different parts of the process.

Is the change working?

We have said already in this article that the change process is ongoing. The train may have left the station but the journey is incomplete. Nevertheless, there are some evaluative judgments that can be made because the new structures are almost at the end of their first full year of operation. Our research with staff members indicates that the change has had a significant impact on daily life for those working in the organisation and that the new structures are seen as "creating opportunities for positive change". The major concerns about organisational and clinical governance have abated and the first eleven months of operation have passed without major difficulties on that front. The key performance indicators have all been met in the first year and this is a major achievement given that this has been achieved with a new team of managers leading a new organisation. Achievements in the first year of operation include:

- integrating a significant element of the disaggregated Argyll and Clyde Health Board into the new, single system structures described above
- continued financial stability including a breakeven plan to resolve the inherited deficit resulting from the merger with Argyll and Clyde
- a successful first annual review highlighting accomplishment of key performance indicators such as waiting times and delayed discharge targets

- solid progress on a major programme of new hospital builds and refurbishments
- launch of a single Board Inequalities Action Plan
- 10 newly established partnership organisations with Glasgow City Council and other local authorities
- a recognised and established approach to organisational development supported by an agreed governance structure and framework
- an established management cohort of over 500 managers with a recognised identity
- a single system approach to corporate planning linked to a structured Individual Performance Management and Development process for managers
- design and development of an innovative online Individual Performance Management and Development system

Conclusions

This article offers a view into one organisation's change challenge. The research conducted with NHS GG&C points to a number of conclusions. First, speed is a relative not an absolute concept when applied to organisational change. A process spanning between one and two years in duration actually felt frenetic. Obviously, factors such as organisational size and complexity play a part in calibrating your thinking about the pace of change. Management teams can become exhausted by the communication and consultation burden that change brings. It is crucial to find creative ways to run day-to-day business whilst simultaneously changing that business. In many ways, these two related but distinct tasks draw on different skill sets and need to be separated for a time at least if the change effort is not to be swamped by daily operational pressures. Using external resources to target specific gaps in expertise can help to maintain momentum, though there are always difficulties with both securing the funds to use external help and in implanting external advisors into complex organisational contexts. Looking beyond the narrow confines of your own organisational setting can offer sources of both reassurance and inspiration. The NHS managers in this project derived real benefits from full and frank discussions with colleagues in other public and private sector organisations. Finally, communication needs to be ongoing and to take into account that different groups in the organisation will perceive the need to change, and whether it is really happening, in different ways. Hence, there is a need for both sophistication (getting the message through to diverse audiences) and directness (sticking to the non-negotiables and driving the change forward when necessary) in leading change. Achieving the most effective balance is the fundamental challenge for those leading and managing change in complex organisations.

References

Bedingham, K./Thomas, T. (2006) Issues in the implementation of strategic change programmes and a potential tool to enhance the process. In: International Journal of Strategic Change Management, 1(1-2): 113–126

Beech, N./Burns, H./de Caestecker, L./MacIntosh, R./MacLean, D. (2004) Paradox as an invitation to act in problematic change situations. In: Human Relations, 57(10): 1313–1332

Dawson, P. (2003) Understanding organisational change: The contemporary experience of people at work. Sage, London

Herrmann, P./Datta, D. K. (2005) Relationships between Top Management Team Characteristics and International Diversification: An Empirical Investigation. In: British Journal of Management, 16(1): 69–78

Kotter, J. P. (1995) The New Rules: How to Succeed in Today's Post-Corporate World. Free Press

Kotter, J. P./Cohen, D. S. (2002) The heart of change. Real life stories of how people change their organisations. Harvard Business School Press, Boston

Lewellyn, S (2001) Two Way Windows: Clinicians as Medical Managers. In: Organisation Studies 22(4), pp. 593–623

MacIntosh, R./Romme, G L (2004) Exploring the Nature of Order Generating Rules. Strathclyde Business School Working Paper, 200403

Taming the lion: How to keep a programme office up and running

Interview with André Krause, O₂ Germany

Since January 2006, the mobile phone company O_2 has belonged to the Spanish company Telefónica – one of the largest globally active telecoms companies. André Krause, now Chief Financial Officer at O_2 Germany, was in charge of the German part of the integration project. In this interview, he summarises his experience as the manager of a programme office.

Telefónica's aim in taking over O_2 was to expand its footprint in continental Europe. The course of the merger was directed by Telefónica's Spanish management and the O_2 Group in London. The formal conclusion of the takeover simultaneously marked the beginning of the integration project during which O_2 was incorporated into the Telefónica group. This created a particular challenge in Germany. Telefónica was little known on the German market. *Telefónica in Deutschland* (Telefónica in Germany) had developed out of mediaWays, a Bertelsmann subsidiary, and HighWay One; it provided DSL infrastructure for Internet service providers (ISPs), voice services as well as other services for business customers.

The mobile provider O_2, by contrast, was one the best-known brands in Germany. The size of the workforce also differed markedly between the two companies: O_2 had about 4,900 employees, compared to only 400 at Telefónica. Together with the headquarters in Spain, therefore, management at O_2 decided in favour of a "reverse takeover" – the integration of German Telefónica into O_2 Germany, while *Telefónica in Deutschland* remained a separate legal entity. It continued to serve third-party customers to make sure that these customers did not buy from its competitor O_2 directly.

In order to optimise the structure of O_2 and *Telefónica in Deutschland* and to benefit from corresponding synergies, however, virtually all the administrative divisions were brought together at O_2. These included Accounting, Controlling, Purchasing and HR. These resources and processes were moved from Telefónica to O$_2$ to realise economies of scale and cut other costs. Depending on the division, this led to savings of between 5 and 30 percent. Furthermore, the business-customer segment was merged and handed over completely to O$_2$. This enabled O$_2$ to extend the integrated range it was already offering private customers, to its business customers.

André Krause, how did you organise the German integration project?

Very quickly, we put together mixed teams with parity representation from both companies and set up a programme office, which, at that time, I headed together with a colleague from Telefónica. We essentially chose the members of top management in the respective divisions to head the individual work streams. We reported to a steering committee made up of the former shareholder Telefónica and our CEO. This committee also took all constitutive decisions.

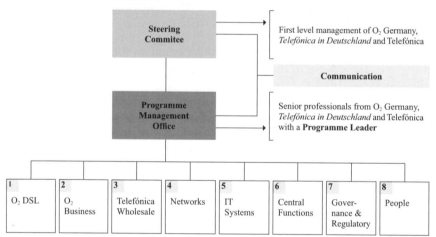

Fig. 1. Structure of the programme office

What were the programme management office's tasks?

During the first project phase we agreed on a strategic approach at the executive management level. What was going to happen? What would move from where to where? Who would be in charge after the change? We decided which divisions were to move to O$_2$, thus laying down a blueprint. In other words, we didn't leave the sections alone with questions like: "Does that make sense now or not?" That would have caused arbitrary discussions leading, perhaps, to the answer: "It's best to leave everything as it is."

How did things continue?

In the second phase, we assigned the job of solving the detailed questions to individual teams – for example, merging processes and standardising IT systems – because you can only achieve the hoped-for economies of scale if you harmonise processes and systems.

Was there a concrete schedule?

The European merger was completed in February 2006; we launched the integration project in Germany in March; and by May/June we had completed the first phase, i.e. we had a rough overall concept. The second phase ran until the end of the summer, although individual integration streams are still working today, because the conversion of IT systems in particular takes time. Then, in August 2006, the colleagues who moved to O_2 during the integration process started to work.

So all in all you had a very tight schedule. Did everything run smoothly?

On the one hand, it was a help to have established clarity relatively quickly. On the other hand, of course, the speed at which we worked also caused problems, because certain things simply cannot be rearranged that quickly and because, at this integration pace, you inevitably lose members of staff.

Does that mean you lost important know-how as well?

We had a disproportionate problem among management and lost some people with know-how, yes. There was simply an unfounded fear among many managers that they would now slip from a good position to the second tier of management. Some of them didn't want to take the risk and preferred to use their good position to make the break.

We tried to identify the key people at an early stage and to keep them on board. For example, we drew up retention packages. But there are always centrifugal forces you cannot control. That is certainly an issue you have to face when you operate at such a speed.

Would you have liked to have had more time?

No. I believe the core benefit is to create security quickly and not to begin a long-drawn-out integration project. Otherwise, performance might suffer. We couldn't afford to let that happen. But in order to maintain the speed, you also have to get infrastructures, processes and systems under control quickly. We didn't always manage this; for example, we had to work with two IT systems in parallel.

Was there a concrete project plan from the outset that you strictly worked through?

During the first three months, the plan was relatively rigid and fixed, and we implemented it quite rigorously – this was also driven by clear-cut deadlines, for example meetings of the steering committee. In the second integration phase, we dissolved the programme office. Speaking from to-day's perspective, that was a mistake and I wouldn't do that the same way again. We had designated the new people for responsible positions, and the idea was that they should now shoulder their responsibility and take over project management. The problem was that this removed some of the pressure, and the day-to-day business displaced the integration tasks from the top of the priority list. That wasn't really supposed to happen, but people are not perfect. For this reason, timelines varied considerably in the second phase. Some projects were implemented more quickly, others more slowly, and some perhaps not at all.

Did this delay have an effect on the business?

This sort of thing only comes to light little by little. For example, after two or three months you find out that the staff are still working with two com-puter screens because the IT systems haven't yet been integrated. This doesn't mean that business operations break down, but the expected syn-ergy and efficiencies aren't felt as soon as you expected.

Staying on the subject of efficiency: did the team members in the programme office continue doing their regular jobs, or were they released from routine business completely?

They were certainly not fully released from their routine business. In both companies, business had to continue, despite the fact that managers also had to cope with integration issues – this took just over a third of their time. During a project period of three months, that adds up to one entire man-month, and I think that's fully sufficient for the conceptual work that had to be done.

Top management later returned from the project structure to working full-time in their functions in the line. Who made the decisions as to which managers – from O₂ or Telefónica – would in the end take over responsibility and the leading positions?

In the great majority of functions it was clear from the outset that O₂ was a much bigger organisation, so that one manager (from O₂) would accordingly become the divisional manager and the other (from Telefónica) the subordinate head of department. Everyone knew from the start that it probably wouldn't happen the other way round. To that extent, there were hardly any disputes over positions.

We have already spoken about the specific situation in Germany with a much larger and stronger O₂. Nevertheless, at the European level, O₂ is the company that has been taken over. Did this context play a role in your project work in Germany?

Not at all. After all, there was no strong *Telefónica in Deutschland* management in Spain. I can't remember any situation in which we had critical discussions or different opinions from Spain. We explained the overall concept very quickly, and that convinced them. No one then got involved in the detailed topics or the implementation.

How did the Telefónica staff in Germany react to this situation?

You need to know that *Telefónica in Deutschland* never operated as part of a major corporate group. They always saw themselves as a medium-sized company; they organised themselves in that way and also acted in that way. To this extent, a critical discussion never arose. Besides, both companies were in a win-win situation. O₂ had always lived under a Damocles sword of uncertainty – are we going to buy someone or are we going to be bought? It was always clear that O₂ Germany was too small from a strategic point of view. Then came the big, protecting hand of the Telefónica group. With Telefónica we had found a safe harbour and could go on operating in peace. The same applied to *Telefónica in Deutschland*, because they were able to slip under O₂'s wing and thus reach a different level of importance and a different focus. Uncertainty became a thing of the past on both sides.

Have O₂ Germany and Telefónica in Deutschland themselves dropped points in the market as a result of focusing so much on themselves?

I would say for the most part no. The wholesale business in a company like Telefónica works with a relatively small number of customers. The customer relations were there, the contracts signed. There was no continuous day-to-day business in which you had to go out and conclude five contracts to generate the desired revenue. At O₂, the entire consumer mobile business was unaffected by the integration. The only area where there were certainly friction losses was the business-customer division. There were problems here: two sales organisations were merged, and we were too preoccupied with ourselves and not enough with the market, the customers and the competition. There's no doubt that we didn't perform 100 percent in this field over a six-month period. But the effect was minimal for the two large divisions, consumer business and the classic wholesale business.

What did you do to maintain motivation in the integration team throughout the three months?

We added a few highlights, had a joint kick-off, and went out for meals together. This enabled the individual managers to "size each other up" for the first time. We tried to dress it all up a little, but there was no classic team building. But then, to be honest, that was not necessary. We didn't exactly have two organisations glaring at each other, armed to the teeth. From the outset, there was a lot of natural cooperation. It's something else when you know you have two redundant organisations that have to find out who is going to survive.

How did you maintain the flow of communication within the virtual team?

Of course it's the programme office's task to define clear reporting procedures, to call for reports and distribute results to maintain a communication flow. We didn't set up any additional information channels apart from that, but also used our standard process-control tools as information tools.

What was your task as programme office manager?

The work involved a combination of administration and content. One essential role that was played by the programme office was to develop the fundamental integration idea, to work out, communicate and coordinate the blueprint and steer it into the individual streams. Then there's always the classic project management – setting milestones, following up deliverables. We also looked at the content that came back from the streams. And whenever we felt the results were not yet good enough, we got involved in content work, challenged it, gave support and tried to ensure the quality as far as we could. Certainly, there are a few more tasks in the field of change management and communications, but we didn't do those ourselves; we brought the corresponding communications department into the team. After all, a total of 200 people moved from Telefónica to O_2. In some cases this involved a physical move, since Telefónica's central office is in Verl, while O_2 has its headquarters in Munich. We had to ensure that the staff didn't get anxious, leading to a decline in performance, but at every second of the integration process they were just as well informed as we wanted them to be. This, too, is the task of the programme office.

How do you assess the fundamental role of internal communications in such a process? When should it begin and what communication tools should be used?

One truism from the entire post-merger business is "communicate quickly". Initially it's not particularly important what you communicate. Rather, the most important thing is to tell people very quickly what is basically happening. Then, when solutions have been developed, you should present them. If you only communicate the process, the results are always unclear and this causes unease. But even that is still better than saying nothing, because then nobody knows what the future holds and everybody ends up talking about everything.

Did you really stick to this principle?

Yes, we communicated very quickly, because we knew that Telefónica would continue to exist in Germany for strategic reasons and that there would also be a wholesale business in the future. We informed top management, and this quickly gave them confidence in the company as a going concern. For most of them, initially it wasn't at all important what this meant in detail. At least they knew that the organisation would continue to exist and that we were planning for growth. In exactly the same way, we were able to tell the staff at O_2, at a very early stage, that the O_2 brand would remain unchanged by integration into the Telefónica group. These statements were very important for the staff. Subsequently, we very quickly explained how the process would look. There then followed three months of project work, and of course there was uncertainty in the divisions affected during this phase. However, it then makes no sense to repeat every day that we haven't made any progress.

What communication formats have proved their worth in this context?

I think it's important to put your faith in personal communication, especially at the beginning and when you're passing on fundamental news. We sent our CEO straight to the Telefónica headquarters in Verl at the outset. We then communicated the CEO's core messages in a top-down manner, cascade-like. We also used classic media – email, intranet, corporate TV, brochures and staff magazines. However, the top decision-makers should always make a personal appearance to pass on the core messages. It isn't the same if a member of staff just reads it somewhere.

What role does top management play in your experience, especially the CEO?

The essential thing is that the CEO is fully aware of his signal effect. If he doesn't radiate the confidence that he knows what he's doing, this will jeopardise discipline in the project. In particular, for such a process, the CEO must follow a very clear, unequivocal course and communicate it emphatically again and again. The topics involved are always critical, and if people pick up the slightest hint of doubt, they will immediately start developing arguments and getting all the mileage they can out of the subject. I believe this is by far the CEO's most important task.

In our specific case, of course, it was also very important to communicate not only into the organisation, but also out of the organisation towards England and Spain, as well as out into the external world. The external world also means "customers", who might be affected. They, too, must be given clarity as quickly as possible on how things are set to continue. Of course, Telefónica's ISP customers called us up the next day, as soon as they read about the merger in the newspaper, to ask whether they would have to look for a new provider. This is also the CEO's responsibility, because a key account team member saying "Don't worry" doesn't help.

Was the integration project threatened by failure at any time?

We had some critical moments. One of these is when you notice that an organisational unit is dragging its feet on really implementing integration, because it isn't certain whether what it is expected to integrate meets its own standards. In this particular case, the team had the feeling they were being expected to build up something that had been going wrong for years. In the programme office you receive all kinds of cover-up arguments in such situations. This is a critical situation, and above all it is very difficult to get the problem out into the open, even when you suspect it. After all, the arguments that are brought forward are usually good, and you have to discuss them even if they are basically only excuses.

How do you react to such situations?

There comes a time when you have to apply pressure. One good example is differences in safety standards. Two systems and organisations face each other and the staff resist all efforts at unification. At some point you can only say: "Sorry, the discussion is over. Decided."

What were the highlights of the project in your view?

One highlight for me was that we already noticed at the first kick-off meeting that the two organisations were very similar – in their way of thinking and in their actions – and that the members of top management were also getting along very well. The integration process would have been much more difficult if that hadn't been the case. Another highlight for me was the day when we welcomed the Telefónica staff members here who had moved to O2. My impression was that they all had a very positive attitude and were looking forward to their work. The third highlight was that all the processes and technicalities worked very well and very quickly.

Retrospectively, how would you assess the project? What lessons can be learned from it?

From the point of view of 100-percent target achievement, it was an 80-percent project. One core reason why it didn't become a 100-percent project was the second integration phase, during which we had dissolved the programme office. Here, we believed too much in the good in people – or rather in managers. The old saying still applies: "Trust, but verify." So we could have been stricter in our implementation. This is a big lesson worth learning, for sure.

Another lesson we learned was in the integration of the business-customer segment. Here, we postponed content until the second phase (i.e. to operational business) which we should have clarified much earlier using a top-down approach. In the meantime, however, service-level agreements have been drawn up and agreed between Telefónica, which maintains the infrastructure, and the business-customer unit, which sells to the end customer.

Otherwise, we got a lot of things right: we were able to rely on the commitment of top management and their involvement; we drew up the concept quickly, launched communications quickly, informed the staff and kept them involved, and didn't waste time by putting off execution. I believe that speed is vital if you want to organise smooth business operations.

André Krause, thank you for this interview.

Beyond

Change before you have to.

Jack Welch, CEO General Electric, 1981–2001

A matter of trust – A journey through the Five Continents of Change Management

Joachim Klewes and Ralf Langen

Today, organisations are in a continuous process of transformation. Change is the norm, not the exception. At the same time, it is becoming increasingly difficult to generate enthusiasm for change and transformation[1] among management, employees and the public. In recent years, it has become significantly harder to make change work. One key component of professional change management is implementing a holistic communications strategy that differentiates between various types of transformation. Here, we liken these types of transformation to expeditions: the organisation is travelling on the route of success, and its possible destinations are the Five Continents of Change. For all these expeditions, Pleon's experience shows trust to be the single most important factor in deciding whether change succeeds or fails.

Over the past decades, there has been no lack of theories about change management and how to cope with the opposition one might encounter within one's own organisation while trying to implement the necessary changes.

Take, for example, the three-stage process model that was originally developed in 1947 by the sociologist Kurt Lewin (Mueller-Stewens and Lechner 2005). Lewin's theory, which represents the traditional school of thought on change management, has been copied or modified by scientists and practitioners ever since.

Basically, the theory states that every organisation passes through three phases during change. The first step is to thaw out existing structures and

---

[1] In this article, the terms "change" and "transformation" are used interchangeably. In the theoretical discussion "transformation" normally refers to long-term holistic change processes whereas "change" constitutes the more comprehensive term and is rather used in context of mergers and acquisitions. In practice Pleon clearly allows for this differentiation. Consequentially, the company's Practice Group is called "Change & Transformation".

processes, to identify and strengthen the drivers for change. The second step is to identify and assess new patterns and to initiate the necessary changes. In the third step, the selected structures, processes and behaviour patterns are fixed. Everyone's common objective is to stabilise the new constellation.

This paradigm, however, has limitations. When it was developed, economic and social structures were much less complex than they are today. Certainly, change was far less prevalent for companies than it is today.

The rules of the game have changed. More than ever, an organisation's ability to change – or even re-invent itself – at ever shorter intervals, has become the key to success. One wave of transformation follows the next, and this is true not only for economic organisations or corporations. These days, government agencies, associations and large NGOs are also chronically 'thawed out'. In many cases, people working in these organisations have already been through several change processes in the past. Some of those people have been actively involved, others less so. Many of them have experienced change either consciously or unconsciously.

There are many reasons why change is becoming increasingly common. According to the German Institute for Economic Research (DIW), these can be clustered into five factors:

1. Individualisation of work environments. Lifelong employment relationships are yielding to more and more flexible employment models. Company workforces are increasingly fluctuating. Consequently, traditional loyalty and motivation mechanisms are on the decline.
2. Shift from manufacturing to services. The services sector is becoming more and more important in the Western industrial nations. The U.S. is still the pacesetter in this development with only one in five employees still working in manufacturing in 2006. This is leading to a workforce that is becoming increasingly better qualified and more sophisticated.
3. Digitalisation and the organisation. Information and communication technologies are rapidly changing workflows and processes. According to BITKOM and Eurostat, fifty percent of employees in Europe were using a computer in 2006. In countries like Denmark, Finland and Sweden there are already clear signs of where the development is heading: in these countries, almost 70 percent of employees are using a PC at work. The effect is that all work and decision-making processes are getting faster and faster.
4. Globalisation of the economy. The volume of world trade – that is, the sum of all imports and exports – more than quintupled from $1.0 trillion in 1980 to $5.5 trillion in 2006 (OECD). In view of growing

competition between countries, high-tech nations like the USA, Japan and Germany are under considerable pressure to innovate. There is much more pressure to adapt quickly to changes on the world market.

5. Demographic changes in society. The structure of populations in the Western industrial nations is changing. The effect: staff – especially qualified staff – will become a scarce resource in the foreseeable future. Migration, the percentage of female employees and the readiness for mobility are all increasing.

Some of these factors have been having an effect and influencing each other mutually for decades already. From a modern point of view, Lewin's three-stages-approach may appear overly simplified and inadequate for describing the change situations organisations now face.

New schools of thought

A more recent and complex theory has been put forward by Harvard professor John Kotter. Like Lewin's model, it has found a wide following, and has been often copied and modified by others. Kotter distinguishes eight stages of change (Kotter 1990):

1. Establish a sense of urgency
2. Create a coalition
3. Develop a clear vision
4. Share a vision
5. Empower people to clear obstacles
6. Secure short-term wins
7. Consolidate and keep moving
8. Anchor the change

According to Kotter, it is crucial that leadership adheres to these stages in the exact same sequence. It is worth noting that this model still assumes that there is a concrete starting point for the process and that the necessary changes need to be anchored in one way or another within the organisation. This seems to be the case with almost all of the procedural approaches (Mueller-Stewens and Lechner 2005).

A less linear approach worth mentioning here is the systems-theory model. It takes account of the dynamic and complex structures found in companies today. Systems theory is based on the idea that systems are self-organising, effectively meaning that change can neither be imposed nor steered fully by management. Instead, leadership has to identify the hidden agendas that drive the day-to-day patterns of interaction within the organisation and that interfere with the necessary changes. With well-placed interventions, these agendas can be invalidated or even enforced, turning those affected in the organisation into active participants. This model has been criticised, among other things, for being prone to manipulations by management and consultants, and for the lack of empirical data to support its theoretical foundations (Mueller-Stewens and Lechner 2005).

Nevertheless, given the growing challenges and continuous changes in their environments, organisations are gradually beginning to realise that they need a different approach to change management. There has also been a gradual shift regarding the role of effective communication in the process and how communication can help to overcome opposition within the organisation. In the early days – this refers to the model put forward by Lewin – communication was mostly regarded as a means of making sense. Employees needed to understand the current situation, the change this necessitated and the way it might evolve over time. In Kotter's model, communication plays a vital part in all of the eight stages, for example, as an intensifier in establishing a sense of urgency.

Today, communication is no longer just a matter of ensuring that a specific change phase is well understood or well established. Rather, it is a means to increase an organisation's systematic ability to change and to master change. In a recent IBM study, 65 percent of the 700 CEOs interviewed said they intended to radically re-organise their company over the following two years (IBM 2006). Considering the large number of smaller change projects that organisations repeatedly undergo, there can only be one conclusion: that change is an ever-present phenomenon that modern organisations can actually instrumentalise to remain permanently on their route of success. With change, companies can generate higher revenues and profits, increase their stability and – through effective communication – create more internal trust and enhance their external reputation.

The IBM study also shows, however, that fewer than half of the CEOs surveyed believe that their companies had successfully mastered change processes in the past. There is no lack of theories and treatises on why changes fail.[2] One of the most common causes seems to be a lack of effort to win internal support. Executive management fails to inform and motivate the entire organisation. How can this be prevented? Professional change management – and this includes communication – can help managers succeed. It is worth remembering, however, that "the employees" are rarely a homogenous group of people. Each individual has his or her own motivations as to why they are part of the company and every employee can contribute to the organisation as a whole in different ways. This, of

---

[2] Paul Crookall and Harvey Schachter (2003), for example, offer a good overview.

course, applies to personnel in change processes – or rather in their opposition to the process – as well.

A metaphorical journey

However, because change is a continuous, ongoing process, even committed executives can easily lose their bearings. What makes things even more difficult is that change has become increasingly differentiated over the past decades – as with almost every social phenomenon. Based on Pleon's experience with change projects, we have condensed the abundance of different change processes into five types. They differ in terms of key parameters and require different change management strategies and, in particular, different approaches to communications. Typically, change becomes necessary if an organisation

- is pursuing a new vision (visionary change),
- is entering a crisis and has to make rapid changes to get out of the crisis (crisis change),
- wants to achieve specific changes in the behaviour of its employees to become a high-performance organisation (energetic change),
- wants to optimise individual processes or structures (procedural change),
- is merging with, or taking over, another organisation (organisational change).

To successfully master their tasks in change management, leadership must therefore first be able to distinguish between the different types of change and understand what the particular demands and opportunities of the actual change situation are. Fundamentally, managers need to focus on and engage every single member of staff: because change is an ongoing process, people will very quickly feel overworked and get frustrated. The following eight questions provide the basis for a quick but reliable check that helps organisations to understand which change situation they are in. The list has proven to be helpful in gaining a more precise understanding of the factors distinguishing the different situations – and strategies – of change:

1. What is the aim of the change?
2. How quickly must change take place?
3. How much uncertainty is there within the organisation?
4. Who decides on the necessary changes?
5. How directly is the leadership involved in the change process?
6. What level of employee involvement is required?

7. How strongly does the change affect the culture of the organisation?
8. What is the most important critical success factor?

It is worth noting that a company may very well find itself in different kinds of change situations at the same time, but it does need to distinguish between them in order to manage the transformation successfully.

Table 1. Variants of change and their characterisation

Change focus	Visionary	Crisis	Energetic	Procedural	Organisational
Aim	Support for new business model	Securing survival	Adaptation of new modes of engagement	Process optimisation	Generating synergies
Time pressure	■	■■■	■■	■■	■■
Uncertainty	■	■■	■	■■	■
Main change driver	CEO plus Board	Board	Board plus next level	Functional C-level plus next level	Steering Committee
Leadership participation	■	■■	■■	■	■■
Employee involvement	■■	./.	■■■	■	■■
Impact on culture	■■	■	■■■	■	■■
Success factors	Coherence of the vision	Central control	Role models	Orientation	Decisiveness

Table 1 distinguishes the five types of change based on the eight criteria mentioned. This is already a highly simplified description of the phenomenon of change. For communication purposes, using metaphors can further reduce the degree of complexity. However, the linguistic image chosen should be highly expressive so that the different forms of change are clearly distinguishable. Hence, the metaphor of Moses planning to lead his people into the land of milk and honey[3] is not very helpful in the majority of change processes. A successful metaphor takes into account, for example, that a change triggered by a crisis will follow a different pattern to a change based on a new corporate vision. There is no ready-made solution.

What could be a suitable metaphor? As described above, organisations share one objective: they want to be successful. They have started out on a journey which, they hope, will lead them to faster growth, higher profits

---

[3] See for example Bernhardt Fischer Appelt: "Die Mose-Methode. Führung zu bahnbrechendem Wandel" (The Moses Method. Leadership to Pioneering Change).

and greater stability. The change process can therefore best be compared with an expedition:

- It has a starting point and a fixed destination.
- The amount of time needed for preparation can vary considerably depending on the kind of task that has been set.
- Resources are finite; they must be purposefully deployed.
- At the same time, a certain amount of leeway must be left for imponderables and unforeseen developments.
- Having the right team often decides the success or failure of the project.
- The project has to be completed within a limited amount of time.
- Progress can be measured in stages.
- Communication plays an important role; it brings the team closer together and helps to uncover friction.

The metaphor of an expedition unifies people and focuses them on the shared objective. Keeping to the metaphor, the change expedition takes us to five different destinations: the Five Continents of Change that represent the five change processes within an organisation mentioned above.

Table 2. Overview of the Five Continents of Change

Focus of Change	Metaphor
Visionary	El Dorado
Crisis	Volcanic Island
Energetic	Olympica
Procedural	Recovery Island
Organisational	United States of Integration

The golden city of El Dorado: Setting out for new horizons

We have been travelling along the river for months now, surrounded by dense jungle. Yesterday we stopped on the riverbank and were promptly ambushed. But I would gladly give my life just for one glimpse of the paradisiacal El Dorado. – Marcos Gonzalez, 1541.[4]

A strong vision can inspire a team to extraordinary achievements. One need only think of the legendary city of El Dorado, which attracted numer-

---

[4] Note: These quotations together with their respective authors are purely fictional. Their only purpose is to add flavour to the metaphors.

ous expeditions in the 16th and 17th centuries. Some people believed they would find an almost Biblical paradise on Earth. Others were primarily lured by the prospect of finding gold. They all were so strongly attracted by the magic of this image that they endured the hardships of the Amazon rainforest.

What applies to expeditions also applies to organisations: the more ambitious the planned project, the more convincingly the leadership must describe the journey's objective. There are many examples of charismatic leaders who use their personality to put an organisation on the right course. Richard Branson of Virgin and Steve Jobs of Apple are certainly among the most prominent. The secret of their success is that they identify themselves absolutely with their company's goals and that, over the past years, they have gained the trust of their employees. For, without trust, no one will follow the leader.

But a company should not rely exclusively on its leadership personality. It also needs a workable idea which develops an internal and an external attraction. At Virgin, this idea is called "non-conformism". 30 years ago, who would have thought that that little record shop would one day run an airline or sell cosmetics, soft drinks and financial services? Today, a colourful collection of virtually unrelated products and services is united under a single brand name. The model seems to work; it can even overcome failures like the Virgin railway line. Virgin sends out internal and external signals suggesting that the company is different from the mainstream – a message that goes down well, at least in the UK. At Apple the vision reads: "Man is the creator of change in this world. As such, he should be above systems and structures, and not subordinate to them." Until 2002, this formula, which was developed decades ago and almost implies an obligation to change, was also expressed in the concise advertising slogan "Think different".

The formulation of a (new) vision to launch many change processes can be organised in very different ways: one possibility is a participatory, exemplary process in which vision, mission and values are defined. Another is the charismatic and trusted corporate leader who determines the direction more or less alone. When it comes to implementing changes, however, there are always five aspects which, in our experience as change consultants, must be given particular attention. First, the vision must fit the actual core business, the portfolio. Second, the strategy must be geared to the vision in a way that people can understand it. Third, the organisational structure must support the vision – across all organisational areas and processes. Fourth, human resources policy must be used as an instrument for implementing the vision. Last but not least, executive management must gain the faith of the employees by setting an example and living both the vision and the related values. By "walking the talk", they enable a corresponding culture to become established in the organisation. Corporate communications must develop and implement strong and effective tools to support this.

Companies that change their business model and give themselves a new vision are setting out on an expedition with an uncertain outcome. Journeys like these may cause uncertainty among participants. Why leave everything behind us if we are still doing so well? Is this the right direction? How much extra effort – or even suffering – will it involve? Will we all really arrive at the destination, or will we have to leave some people behind? These feelings must be taken into account when developing the vision and the related change strategy. The following aspects of visionary change may help in this:

- The aim of the vision is to improve the organisation's own capacity for innovation.
- The staff must be allowed to take personal initiative and have an opportunity to learn.
- Its implementation initially has only a minor effect on the daily work routine and (if applicable) on the behaviour of the capital market. It will, however, very probably be noticed by the media and by consumers.
- The authenticity of the organisation must be ensured.

Fleeing from a volcanic island: change in a crisis

The outbreak of the volcano in the center of the country came as a complete surprise to us. Some of my best men have been killed by lava. We only have a few hours left to evacuate the defenceless population. I have already put a team together who will be organising the boats. What we lack is a good plan. One question torments me in particular: will this idyllic island ever recover from this catastrophe and give us a home again? – Author unknown

75,000 years ago, the eruption of the volcano Toba on the Indonesian island of Sumatra spewed more than one billion tons of ash and sulphur gases into the atmosphere. This event accelerated the cooling of earth, lowering worldwide temperatures by as much as 15 degrees Celsius. It is a widely held theory among scientists that the Toba eruption sent humanity to the brink of extinction. Events like this and their after-effects are virtually impossible to predict – this is also true for many dangerous situations organisations will eventually face: product-quality incidents, accusations of corruption against the executive personnel, natural disasters that destroy most of the company's assets – the list of conceivable critical situations is almost endless. A crisis can hit anytime, just as a volcanic eruption on a South Sea island catches the participants of an expedition unprepared.

Let us look at one example here, too. When terrorists attacked the World Trade Center in New York, and destroyed one of the American symbols of economic success, on September 11, 2001, people all over the world were shocked. As we all know, the consequences of this event were far-reaching and affect us to this day. Following the attack, airline companies suffered from an immediate lack of business. People all over the world felt insecure travelling by plane. One of the leading European airline companies, French-Dutch KLM, entered a serious crisis that it could not possibly have predicted beforehand. Management was forced to act. It immediately launched "Operation Baseline", a short term cost-control initiative with only one aim: ensuring the company survived. Operation Baseline contained measures like ceasing recruitment, ending all financial obligations that did not contribute to the primary business, freezing activities like the introduction of an intranet, and so on. Operation Baseline was understood by all staff, there was no discussion about the necessity and there was a strong support in the organisation. Employees had strong faith in the measures that were taken. In the end, KLM survived.

Ideally, an organisation has resilient structures and flexible processes enabling it to react in a unified and united way. This is also where a systematically established crisis prevention system proves its importance. Companies should know at all times how they are perceived by the public. They need to identify relevant developments regarding their core business. Additionally, an organisation that communicates with different stakeholders on a regular basis, such as journalists or politicians, will find it much easier to cooperate with them during a crisis. A tried-and-tested issues-management system that is continuously monitoring everything that is relevant to the company can also help in a change process, for example. Stability in the face of a crisis and an ability to transform are thus inseparably connected.

Change processes during a crisis – or triggered by a crisis – have several special characteristics. Here are some of them (by way of example):

- The onset (and often the duration) of the change process are determined externally.
- The pressure to change is high.
- The executive level of management will normally decide on, and implement, the necessary measures quickly in order to prevent damage to the company and its reputation.
- Depending on the extent of the crisis, the change process will have a very strong effect on everyday work.

- The capital market – as well as other stakeholders, for example in the political arena – will monitor the organisation's behaviour very closely – and punish every mistake.

As is the case with fleeing from a volcanic island, there is little time for discussion in a crisis. The process has to be executed with virtually military precision. The more willingness and ability to change there already is in an organisation, and the higher the level of trust, the more likely it is that the organisation will get through the crisis intact.

Olympica: Not doing everything differently, but with much more energy

Ahead of us lies the legendary island of Olympica. I can hardly believe it. At last the hardship of the last few months are paying off and we will soon be among the best of the best. The officers and crew will not shrink from any effort to work for the benefit of our expedition and will truly surpass themselves. Undreamt-of wealth will be our reward. – Spiros Enceladus, 500 BC

There once was a mythical island named Olympica – or at least that is what we would like to call it. Its utopian society strived for perfection at all costs and was open to those who were willing to do the same and sacrifice their established ways. The aim here is to be ahead in all disciplines. Whoever gets behind has to suffer the consequences and leave. Who would want to live on an island as elitist as this? Well, let us just say that the pay-off is very much worth the trouble. Not only do Olympicans live in prosperity. They are highly regarded and treated with respect, wherever they travel.

Many organisations claim that they are travelling to Olympica, in modern terms usually described as "high performance organisation". But they forget that here, too, the journey is the destination. Changing the "energy level", the commitment and attitudes of staff is one of the most difficult change processes. In our everyday lives we have all heard phrases like: "We've always done things this way here", or know of attitudes towards service or quality that are not acceptable for customers or business partners. Companies thus often have good reasons for changing their staff's attitude or even the corporate culture. An almost standard example is the huge transformation of the former monopolistic companies in the telecommunications and energy industries all over Europe as a result of competition. In many cases, management has failed to train or sensitise the workforce properly up to now. A typical example of this is the service offensive announced by Deutsche Telekom's CEO René Obermann in late

2006. The aim, he said at the time, was to make the company more cus-tomer-friendly and competitive. Had the former state monopolist missed an important development? Whatever the reason, the proposal to move much of the workforce into the group's own service company led to a strike that lasted several weeks. Here and elsewhere, strong trade unions have meant that parts of the workforce are not as flexible as the global market requires.

Here is another example: the second-largest credit insurance company in the world, Atradius, decided to further develop its strategic positioning in order to create a powerful and differentiated positioning in the market place. Unsurprisingly, Atradius quickly realised that it needed to get its people on board in order to really deliver its new positioning to its custom-ers and external stakeholders. With this realisation, the management launched an internal campaign aimed at involving staff in contributing to its new message. Starting in the Netherlands, Atradius organised an am-bassador programme that involved ten percent of the employee population in workshops. Here, they were given the opportunity to discuss new ways of working that would then strengthen the company's organisational cul-ture and help them deliver on the promises being made to external stake-holders. Representatives from the management team were also involved, knowing that many decisions would need to be made in order to imple-ment the ideas raised by the ambassadors. The newly found commitment to company initiatives, including reconsidering its organisational structures in order to facilitate and improve internal cooperation in the customers' in-terests, is now part of the company ethos.

There are some important lessons in this example that apply to almost all change processes that aim to change the behaviour of employees. First and foremost: describe the desired result as vividly as possible and find role models who are living or willing to live in the desired manner. A smart way to do this in communications is to embed the desired behaviour in stories – stories are much more compelling than information. Another key factor, in successfully changing people's behaviour, is incentives. This does not simply mean penalties for those who deviate from the path. A positive reward system can be a very effective means of change as well.

Companies who want to reach the island of Olympica should bear in mind the following points on their expedition:

- A high level of "energy" and performance is required of every member of staff, but most of all of top management. Here, too, there is nothing stronger than an effective role model.
- The aim must be to promote personal initiative, a culture of open inter-action and mutual respect, and to advance specialist training.

- Behaviour relating to goals must be clearly described and defined – ambiguity is harmful.
- Nothing will be achieved unless the intended behavioural change is broken down to the level of concrete work situations. Just as the top level of management is needed to decide on the content and pace of change, middle and lower management are just as important as promoters of change.

In the expedition to Olympica, everyone has to continuously review their own performance and abilities – be it alone or with the help of external specialists. External specialists can prepare the way for an urgently needed change of perspective and provide an external view of the company. However, for all its efforts to achieve perfection, a company must never lose sight of the objective of remaining authentic. This applies just as much to behavioural change as to visionary change.

Recovery Island: Process optimisation as a principle

We found out today that we are not the only ones who have gone off in search of the riches. Unfortunately, the other expeditions always seem to be slightly ahead of us. What can be the explanation? To be on the safe side we head for the nearest port and have our ship modernised. – David James Scott, 1832

Every now and then, depending on the scope of the journey, an expedition has to have a stopover, be it to gather new resources, or to repair or even improve the equipment and the ship. A lot of them choose Recovery Island as their destination. This somewhat mysterious place not only has a lot to offer in terms of resources. It also allows expeditions to continue their journey, admittedly with less speed, while they are still experimenting with their equipment. A paradox? Not really.

As is the case for expeditions, no company can afford to stand still today. If you want to hold your own against the competition you have to constantly optimise your processes. And precisely such improvements of individual processes or functions are the primary focus of this variant of change management. The issue here is the continuous optimisation of work patterns, structures and functions – from streamlining the workflow to adjusting a sales organisation or outsourcing the HR function to a shared service centre. Technical innovations offer some of the most important opportunities for optimisation. At the beginning of this article, digitalisation was cited as one of the key drivers of change. This means more than opening an online shop and selling products via the Internet. Digitalisation is penetrating every aspect of day-to-day corporate life. Most business processes can be handled electronically today, leading to optimised and more efficient workflows and so improving the bottom line.

Developments in today's retail trade typify the current digital revolution. Several major groups, including Wal-Mart in the USA, Tesco in the UK and the Metro Group in Germany, have decided to introduce what is known as radio frequency identification (RFID) into their logistics systems. RFID is a technology that makes it possible for product and process data to be transmitted simply by radio. Up until now, the bar code, which is still printed on the packaging of every product today, has been used in this field. But unlike bar codes, the information on RFID chips no longer has to be scanned by hand by store staff. Data for entire truckloads of products can be processed into the IT system in a few minutes. The process improvement is enormous, as is the savings potential.

What the retailers did not consider was how long it would take the staff to get used to the new processes resulting from the technology. The introduction of new technologies creates a lot of uncertainty for staff. For example, if all the purchases can be captured by radio, it is possible that people will no longer be needed to staff the cash desk in the future. So any member of staff who promotes the introduction of the new technology might feel they are putting their own job at risk and – in the final analysis – making themselves redundant.

It is the task of management to give the staff an urgently needed sense of security and confidence as they face new developments. Above all, it is important to give the staff some prospects for the future. What will be their role in the changed system? For this reason, the retail companies mentioned in this article have prepared extensive programmes for internal communication and staff training to accompany this technological change. They do not hide the fact that reduction of staff will be unavoidable in certain departments, but they also point out solutions at the same time. Through constant communications they establish a level of confidence that helps to introduce the technology. As regards the execution of the change process, it has proven helpful to create alliances, either within the company itself – the IT department, for example – or if the necessary resources are lacking, with external partners. A pilot should be run before the final roll-out of new technologies or processes. This allows for a re-evaluation and, if necessary, further adjustment. Management must keep in mind that there is no out-of-the-box solution: every system has to be tailored exactly to the specific needs of the organisation. For communication purposes, the procedural change may be put into a larger context: for example, positioning the company as being especially innovative or ecologically-minded.

What do organisations that put in an intermediate stop on Recovery Island have to look out for?

- First, they must clearly define the desired results. For example, the efficiency gains, greater process flexibility and the prospect of better-quality and more innovative products must be described as vividly as possible.
- The change has the strongest impact on the foundation ("backbone") of the company: this can well lead to friction with the parts of the company that work most directly with customers.
- More than other change categories, this conversion can be covered using the terms and methods of project management, so that its beginning and end can be precisely specified.
- The initiators of the process are often frontline managers and the staff themselves.

United States of Integration: Melting pot of cultures

Our leader has gotten hold of three weird guys somewhere in this port who are supposed to reinforce our crew. They say they are unbeatable when it comes to finding food. Yet the guys don't even speak our language, they walk in a funny way and wear strange clothes. I keep well out of their way and always sleep with a knife under my pillow. – Conroy O'Hara

Imagine that the expedition crew finds itself on an unknown island and has to form an alliance with the natives in order to survive – either voluntarily or by force. If a certain goal cannot be reached by itself, expedition parties are well advised to seek out partners that possess the much-needed skills: two or more communities that used to act autonomously now come together to form a single unit. The role model for this would not be the European Union, where the cultural differences are still very marked and one does not always get the impression that everyone is speaking with one voice. Rather, the model is the USA, where many cultures merge into one, leading to something new and original. Like the USA, the United States of Integration is more than the sum of its parts.

Corporate takeovers or mergers are certainly some of the most spectacular examples of change processes. Spectacular because they usually affect the entire company and staff and are therefore followed attentively by the public. Also, the striking monetary sums involved add to the heightened awareness: According to Thomson Financial, in the first half of 2007 alone, the value of worldwide mergers and acquisitions totalled $2.39 trillion – 46 percent more than in the previous year.

What factors influence the success of the United States of Integration? First, the union must make sense economically. That is, there must be synergies, be it from sharing the same resources or from improved purchasing terms. Take, for example, the takeover of the international cosmetics company Wella AG by industry giant Procter & Gamble in 2003. Both companies were leading players in the field of professional hair care, and their businesses were highly complementary. In this case, Wella's strengths and experiences even enhanced P&G's growth potential in this particular field of beauty care. The mid-term synergy potential was estimated to be approximately €300 million a year – no small amount, even at a purchase price of €4.65 billion. However, some concerns had to be met before the deal could be closed. Namely, there was initial opposition and even distrust on behalf of Wella's management as well as labour representatives, who had not been involved in the sales process of the largely family-owned company. Other topics that had to be addressed included the employees' fears of job cuts, restructuring and relocations, and public opposition of losing a German company to US-based P&G. Eventually, the takeover was accomplished by a carefully considered strategy which involved information as well as confidence-building and corporate storytelling.

This example shows that in most cases the human factor is one of the most important aspects determining the success of integration projects, even before the actual process has started. Empirical studies have shown that integration projects often fail because managers and employees simply do not understand why they should give up something that they have learned, that they have confidence in and that has proven its worth. The advice would be to act resolutely. Power structures and accountabilities should be laid out so that quick wins can be achieved. Concentrate on small projects that can serve as a template for success stories and that can be used in communications. One has to keep in mind, though, that integration processes usually last a long time. What management ideally wants to achieve is a large percentage of employees taking individual responsibilities and furthering the change process. Also, the focus should not be put exclusively on internal processes but on external communications as well, creating public trust and support for the merger in the process. This will, in turn, positively affect the acceptance of the change within the organisation.

What do companies have to look out for when creating the United States of Integration?

- Communication should start straight after the announcement of the integration as a loss of trust and value can already emerge during negotiations and antitrust examinations. Thus, the legal scope has to be considered.

- Upon completion, the integration process has to be sped up by the project management office,[5] which should be established exclusively to account for this process. Studies show a positive correlation between the fast implementation of the communications strategy and the development of management ratios such as productivity and profitability.[6]

- Companies have to balance their revenue and cost initiatives. Instead, many companies try to find cost-reducing synergies first and lose sight of their regular business and existing customers. Also, competitors might increasingly go on the offensive during this process.

- While the management board and shareholders are drivers for M&A, the middle management and employees are often not involved. Line managers especially fear losing their positions. As they are simultaneously the most important sources of information for employees, it is crucial to convince and empower the leadership populations to support the change.

- The integration of corporate cultures should be based on a cultural audit of all affected cultures and be implemented mainly through the participation of leadership teams and employees.

At the end of the journey

The expedition metaphor should not create the impression that an organisation cannot master more than one of the above-mentioned change processes at the same time. There are often several changes – sometimes overlapping – taking place within an organisation at the same time. One good example is the Japanese group Nissan, which the French carmaker Renault bought for €5.4 billion in 1999. Nissan was economically on the ropes when the new manager Carlo Goshn took over. He broke all the taboos of Japanese corporate culture, for example by firing thousands of employees. He cut ties with hundreds of component suppliers and got rid of almost the entire product range. Nissan was engaged in creating the United States of Integration; at the same time it was on Recovery Island, the Island Olympica and en route for El Dorado.

Even so, the metaphors are still helpful in finding one's bearings when trying to come to terms with a current change situation. This is because they make it easier to distinguish between the different types of change and make processes less complex, even if only for discussions and for

---

[5] The function of the project management office is also described in the interview with André Krause in this volume.
[6] See Pricewaterhouse Coopers (1997) and Albizzatti, Christofferson et al. (2005).

planning the change. For, just as there is no single change process, there is no ready-made solution for change management. The necessary measures have to be re-compiled individually again and again.

Talking about change – The communications approach

The metaphor of the Five Continents of Change helps companies choose the appropriate communications strategy for their individual situation – as an integral and essential part of the overall change strategy. For this, the people in charge need to take into account the desired results, or more precisely, the desired outcome among leaders and employees. In his research into how organisations are engaging their staff in developing change, John Smythe has identified four different communication approaches that lead to four different outcomes (Smythe 2004). For example, leaders who "tell the many what has been decided by the few" will find that this forces the majority of their staff into spectator mode, denying them the experience of actively participating in the change process. This may sound like communications from a bygone era, but is really a viable alternative in specific change situations, namely when a company needs to leave Volcanic Island as quickly as possible. At KLM, management knew what was needed in the 9/11-aftermath and the message it sent was clearly understood by all target groups: "Don't worry, we're in control." Strong leadership with clear communications via all channels helped in building trust not only with staff, but with the capital market and the customers as well.

According to Smythe, most leaders tend to choose an approach that he describes as "selling to the many what has been decided by the few", resulting in compliant collaborators in the staff. This might sometimes work within the context of Olympica, where employees need to be motivated in order to achieve the desired level of engagement. But leadership must keep in mind that the mere launching of a change initiative does not automatically bring it to life on an operational level. The message that has been sent needs to be consistently followed through for a significant period of time.

The third approach Smythe identifies as "driving accountability down". Here, individual employees are involved in the change process and given the time to apply the decisions to their own work. As the example above of insurance company Atradius has shown, this works very well within the context of Olympica. With its ambassadors, Atradius had a large enough group of willing collaborators who furthered the process. The involvement of employees is always a good choice when their input is needed to achieve a certain goal, for example process optimisation. On Recovery Island, people will feel valued and more secure if their opinion is heard and acted upon.

The fourth approach is what Smythe calls "co-creation". This engages people who will add value to a certain decision or change strategy, for example, because they provide a new perspective, or because they are recognised by the employees who eventually will implement the change. In the examples above, this would be the Change Champions of the United States of Integration. But it is quite obvious that this approach should be considered with all Five Continents of Change, although the affected groups may differ in size and seniority.

In choosing their communications approach, management must, more than anything else, consider the level of trust it helps to establish. Our journey along the Five Continents of Change has shown the importance of employees' faith in their leadership as a "common denominator" in all types of change. Be it a new vision, in times of crises, a new level of engagement, better processes, or in mergers and acquisitions: trust is paramount for success. This can only be established through constant and holistic communications. In change situations, employees as well as external target groups will remember the way management has acted in the past and build their opinion on that. For some organisations, this might be a boon. For others, this will even add to the opposition they have to face during the change process. Therefore, reputation management plays a vital part in change communications, and vice versa.

A word on tools

From a communications point of view, choosing specific communication tools for change-related reputation management is not as important as selecting the right communications strategy. Standard communication tools, which are well established within the company, should always be used, but not exclusively. Of course, certain tools are not suited to the quick response generally needed in change situations. This applies especially to the so-called standard communications tools (if these are not explicitly modified and adapted to the purpose)[7]. For example, a bi-monthly employee magazine is definitely not the right channel if you want to spread your messages quickly and to the point. Also, standard tools do not generate the level of attention often required in order for change communications to reach everyone who is affected. Therefore, unorthodox multi-directional

---

[7] See Markus Pickel's contribution in this volume.

channels, which offer a means of feedback, should be chosen. For some technically oriented organisations, Web 2.0 applications might work – but ideally, the communications channels should allow for face-to-face interaction, where employees can experience their management authentically. We strongly believe that new tools for communications, like word-of-mouth techniques, are promising for change management, but their potential has yet to be fully tapped. However, one thing is certain: communications that informs, explains, provides orientation and involves is a key success factor for change management.

Choosing the right communications tools is certainly important. But the success of communications during a change "expedition" depends more on the communications strategy. In particular, the following questions[8] about communication strategies have to be answered:

- What specific goals should communication achieve in the various phases of the change process?
- Which target groups have to be accentuated and how can communications be focused on these particular target groups?
- Which channels and means will be used to transmit the messages?
- How much bi-directionality between transmitters and receivers should communications encourage or allow?
- What communicative messages and topics are suitable?

The answers to these questions depend very much on the type of change involved. Here are some examples (by no means an exhaustive list):

- Communication goals:[9]
  For change situations triggered by a crisis (metaphorically, fleeing from Volcano Island), information and behaviour-related communications goals are more important than those relating to attitudes and sensibilities. Here, communication goals are typically much more concrete than, say, in change processes that are triggered by visions that originate in top management and filter through to the various management levels.

---

[8] The presented selection of potential tasks for communications strategies is by no means exhaustive.

[9] We define communication goals as unambiguous statements about what specific target groups should know at a defined point in time ("information goals"), what precise attitude they should have ("attitude goals"), or what behaviour they should exhibit ("behavioural goals"). Communication goals in this sense always relate to precisely identified recipients and to precise points in time. They detail the over-arching strategic goals that an organisation would like to achieve through communications.

- Target-group-specific emphases:
  Clearly, communication in change processes has to speak to all groups in an organisation. Certainly, one of the biggest mistakes in change situations is to underestimate the importance of external reputation and see change as an internal matter. The expedition to Recovery Island, with its focus on process optimisation, certainly makes it possible to concentrate on internal target groups, or even specific parts of the organisation – such as the employees and "internal customers" of the IT division, if it is the IT division whose processes are being optimised. That communications during different phases of a change process can emphasise different target groups is well-known. Most ideas about cascading communications are based on this. But even how much this emphasis is shifted depends on the change type. During the escape from Volcano Island, or the journey to the United States of Integration, for example, all internal target groups must be reached much more quickly and more broadly than for other change types.

- Transmitter communication:
  The change type also determines the choice of transmitter: whether, for example, the CEO will always be the most suitable transmitter for communication[10], or whether change agents or multipliers[11], or even external "authorities" are more suitable. For example, it often makes sense for energetic change (the journey to Olympica) and process-optimising change (Recovery Island) to use top management only at certain points, or to keep them as a communications reserve, since specialists or informal authorities in smaller organisational units may appear more credible as transmitters.

- Bi-directionality:
  Perhaps the clearest case for using top-down change-related communication is during crisis-induced change. Visionary change, too, usually admits little bi-directionality – at least, in the initial phases. Here, however, a bottom-up component must emerge, at least symbolically, when an explicit corporate vision is being developed and the blueprint is not provided by a charismatic leader or owner. For all change types, however, the degree of bi-directional communication should increase as the change process develops.

- Messages of communications:
  Here, too, there are differences depending on the change type. For example, creating an almost religious conviction that change is necessary (already a specific set of messages) is most important for energetic

---

[10] See Robert Wreschniok's contribution in this volume.
[11] See Eike Wagner's contribution in this volume.

change (Olympica) and integration processes. This explicit message is unnecessary for crisis-induced change and visionary change, where the new business model or the new technological direction themselves exert a certain fascination or magnetism. It is surely the greatest challenge in any change process to devise messages that not only appear necessary from the viewpoint of top management, but that are also highly credible from the viewpoint of employees.

The interrelationships discussed here between these aspects of communication and change types are only examples. But they reflect Pleon's experience, namely: finding the right combination of answers for each change type – essentially, developing the communication strategy – is not a question of deducing a result from a (rather meagre) set of "theories". Furthermore, in the change processes guided by Pleon, the strategies developed in a strategic discourse – which, certainly, must be systematically structured – have proven much superior to those derived, however rigorously, from fragments of theories.

The metaphorical illustration of the change types (through the expeditions to the five continents of change) is in fact valuable because it enables top management and communication experts, when developing these strategic discourses, to understand each other and to creatively deploy standard solutions.

Godspeed!

The most important piece of information comes at the end: expeditions can always fail. In the same way, every change process involves risks for each of the groups involved. Still, how would our modern map look without the expeditions of the past? And how can organisations be expected to adapt to changes in their environmental conditions without systematic change processes? Change is a necessary and continuous process. The motto must be: take the initiative. Those who are well prepared for expeditions will be successful – regardless of which continent of change they are headed for.

References

Albizzatti, Nicolas J./Christofferson, Scott A./Sias, Diane L. (2005) Smoothing postmerger integration. In: The McKinsey Quarterly, September 2005

Crookall, Paul/Harvey Schachter, Harvey (2003) Changing Management Culture: Models and Strategies to Make It Happen. http://www.tbs-sct.gc.ca/cmo_mfc/Toolkit2/GCC/cmc_e.pdf (as of: Nov. 2007)

IBM (2006) Global CEO Study. http://www-935.ibm.com/services/us/gbs/bus/ html/bcs_ceostudy2006.html?re=bcsstrategychange (as of: Nov. 2007)

Kotter, John P. (1996) Leading Change. Harvard Business School Press, Boston

Müller-Stewens, Günter/Lechner Christoph (2005) Strategisches Management. Wie strategische Initiativen zum Wandel führen (in German). Schäffer-Poeschel, Stuttgart

Pricewaterhouse Coopers (1997) Speed Makes the Difference: A Survey of Mergers & Acquisitions.

Smythe, John (2004) Engaging people at work to drive strategy and change. Research into how organisations are engaging their leaders and employees in developing strategy and change which points to a growing belief in the value of an inclusive approach. Version 4 non participants. http://www.engageforchange.com/engagement/articles/index.html (as of: Oct. 2007)

About the authors

Nic Beech is a Professor of Management at the University of St Andrews. His research is focused on the social dynamics of organisational life – the intertwining of people's identities, relationships and practices. He has a particular interest in creative industries and the health sector. Nic has published five books on these topics.

Peter Fischer is a Senior Lecturer at the University of Exeter, UK. His research interests are economic and organisational psychology, information processing in decision-making, aggressive behaviour as well as health psychology.

Dieter Frey is a Professor of Social Psychology at the Ludwig-Maximilians-University Munich. Since 2003, he has been Academic Director of the Bavarian Elite Academy. His research focuses on decision behaviour, preconditions of innovation, teamwork, leadership, and the emergence and changes of attitudes and value systems. His main focus is to interconnect theory and practice and to facilitate the transfer between academia and industry.

Marit Gerkhardt received her doctorate in an in-service programme of the BMW Group Change Management Consultancy and the Ludwig-Maximilians-University Munich. Since 2007, she has worked as an independent management consultant focusing on change management.

John-Philip Hammersen has been Press Relations Officer and Director External Communications at the Bundesagentur für Arbeit (BA), the German Federal Employment Agency, since July 2005. Before, he worked as an editor for several daily newspapers, including Die Welt and BILD, as Head of News for the RTL-Group and as Editor in Chief for one of the biggest TV production networks in Germany. As a freelance consultant, John-Philip assisted in the launch of a regional TV station and the daily paper "NEWS Frankfurt".

Ulrich Kallmeyer is Chairman of the Radeberger Gruppe KG's board of directors. Since 1985 he has held numerous executive positions at board level in companies within the Oetker Group. After attaining his degree in business economics at the University of Hamburg, he started his career at Unilever in Hamburg.

Joachim Klewes is Senior Partner of Pleon and co-founder of the public relations consulting firm Kohtes Klewes. His expertise includes major national and international assignments in the fields of corporate communications, communications management as well as corporate change and crises. Outside of Pleon, he has held managerial positions on a national and international level. He is an Associate Professor at the Freie Universität Berlin, founding partner of the opinion research institute com.X in Bochum and a frequent writer, publisher and speaker on communications subjects.

Paul J. Kohtes is co-founder of the public relations consulting firm Kohtes Klewes, now Pleon. In 2006, he became the first German to be admitted to the 'Hall of Fame' of the ICCO. Today, he conducts seminars in Zen meditation and specialises in the coaching of executive managers. In 1998, he founded the Identity Foundation, a non-profit foundation researching the topic of identity, together with his wife Margret Kohtes.

André Krause is the Managing Director of Finance of O_2 (Germany). Before joining O_2 in 2004, he worked for McKinsey & Company and Arthur Andersen with a focus on IT, computer risk management and auditing.

Rainer Lang is Senior Consultant and head of Pleon Research and Evaluation, in Bonn. His work focuses on the measurement of the value proposition of communication, and media and reputation analyses, as well as on the development of issues management systems. After completing a degree in macroeconomics, he worked for several research institutes in the fields of applied and empirical economic research.

Ralf Langen is Managing Partner of Pleon Germany and European Head of Pleon's Change & Transformation Practice, based in Munich. He has been a communications management professional for more than 15 years both on the industry side and as a consultant. Ralf specialises in change management, and crisis and issues management. He is also the founder and chairman of the European Centre for Reputation Studies (ECRS).

Robert MacIntosh holds a Chair in Strategic Management at the University of Glasgow and is a chartered engineer. He has researched strategic change in a variety of public, private and voluntary sector organisations for over 15 years. Robert also publishes on research methods and practitioner relevance.

Eric Meyer is Manager of the Institute for Business Cooperation at the University of Münster. He studied mathematics at the University of Oldenburg and joined the institute in 2004.

Markus Pickel, PhD and DVM, is Head of Global Corporate Communications of Bayer HealthCare and has significant experience of various management positions in the pharmaceutical and chemical industries. He has managed large change programs in the area of business process reengineering, change leadership and restructuring as well as in the field of M&A.

Katrin Schwabe is Business Director of Pleon's Change & Transformation Unit in Munich. She focuses on designing dialogue solutions that support large-scale change communication efforts. She has consulted a number of global organisations in cultural change processes, alignment towards a new strategic direction and the implementation of a new values system. Prior to joining Pleon, she worked for international consulting firms specialising in learning and change management.

Sabine Stecher is Consultant in the Change and Transformation team at Pleon. Before joining the agency, she was Consultant and Group Head with JPKOM in Düsseldorf and Frankfurt, an agency specialising in change and corporate communications. After completing her MA in German philology, social psychology and theatre at Ludwig-Maximilians-University in Munich, Sabine worked as an editor for the news magazine Focus, the national newspaper Süddeutsche Zeitung and the broadcaster Bayerischer Rundfunk.

Theresia Theurl is Professor of Economics at the University of Münster. She received her PhD at the University of Innsbruck. She joined the University of Münster in 2000 and is Director of the university's Institute for Business Cooperation. Her research interests focus on the management of business co-operation.

Eike Wagner works as a freelance consultant and trainer and is a lecturer for personnel management at the University of Applied Sciences, Kempten. Before this, he worked for three years in the central change management consultancy of BMW group. Eike studied economics at the University of Applied Sciences in Paderborn and holds a PhD from Oxford Brookes University.

Robert Wreschniok is a Senior Consultant, specialising in reputation management and integrated communication. He is a member of the board of the European Centre for Reputation Studies. After completing his MA in international relations at the University of Sussex (UK), he joined Pleon in 2002. In 2005, he completed the Programme in Strategic Foundation Management at the University Basel (Switzerland) and became spokesperson for the Private Institute for Foundation Law, based in Munich and Berlin.

Julia Zangl is responsible in the field of market and opinion research at Pleon Research and Evaluation. The main focus of her job is to conduct national and international surveys focusing on PR evaluation and stakeholder communication. Julia holds a degree in public relations and studied sociology, law, and German language and literature.

Index